Gibraltar 1779–83

The Great Siege

Campaign • 172

Gibraltar 1779–83

The Great Siege

René Chartrand · Illustrated by Patrice Courcelle

First published in Great Britain in 2006 by Osprey Publishing,
Midland House, West Way, Botley, Oxford OX2 0PH, UK
44-02 23rd St, Suite 219, Long Island City, NY 11101, USA
Email: info@ospreypublishing.com

Osprey Publishing is part of the Osprey Group.

Transferred to digital print on demand 2011

First published 2006
1st impression 2006

Printed and bound by PrintOnDemand-Worldwide.com, Peterborough, UK

A CIP catalogue record for this book is available from the British Library

ISBN: 978 1 84176 977 6

The author, Rene Chartrand, has asserted his right under the Copyright, Designs and Patents Act, 1988,
to be identified as the Author of this Work.

Design by Mark Holt
Maps by The Map Studio
3d bird's-eye views by Origin3D Ltd
Battlescene artwork by Patrice Courcelle
Index by Glyn Sutcliffe
Originated by United Graphics, Singapore
Typeset in Helvetica Neue and ITC New Baskerville

Author's note

The American War of Independence was disastrous for Britain. Its political and diplomatic efforts failed while its armed forces
suffered many setbacks at the hand of the French, Americans and Spaniards. Through all the depressing war dispatches came
the incredible resistance of the garrison of Gibraltar against enormous odds. The Great Siege of Gibraltar was a notable event in
British and in world history. It buoyed the British people, proving its valour during a dark hour of its long history, while showing the
world that its spirit was invincible. In British hearts to this day, the Great Siege made Gibraltar – in spite of the distance – a proud
part of the realm, an extension of the White Cliffs of Dover or of the Scots Highlands. As will be seen in this book, it was a well-
earned distinction that was won against a tenacious and resourceful enemy.

The author wishes to acknowledge the very kind assistance of James L Kochan, Stephen Wood, Peter Harrington of the
Anne SK Brown Military Collection, the staff of the Public Records Office at Kew, the Gibraltar Museum and of the Museo Naval
in Madrid. Commissioning Editor Alexander Stilwell turned our masses of notes and files into an attractive imprint.

The Woodland Trust
Osprey Publishing is supporting the Woodland
Trust, the UK's leading woodland conservation
charity, by funding the dedication of trees.

www.ospreypublishing.com

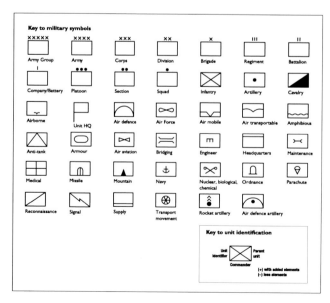

CONTENTS

INTRODUCTION

The Atlantic Ocean is connected with the Mediterranean Sea by a narrow channel, the Straits of Gibraltar, one of the globe's most important geographical features. To the north, the Iberian peninsula in Europe; to the south, the North African coast. On the Atlantic, the most southerly point of the peninsula is the town of Tarifa, in the kingdom of Spain. From its point, one can clearly see the busy harbour of Tangier, in the kingdom of Morocco.

Since ancient times, the Straits have marked the border between Europe and Africa and have been recognized to be of prime strategic importance. Whoever controlled the Straits controlled the movement between the two continents and held the key to invading armies and fleets to either Europe or Africa.

Just east of the Atlantic entrance of the Straits, on the European shore, a magnificent and huge 'rock' can be seen on a peninsula facing

The Straits of Gibraltar as seen from high up on the 'Rock' of Gibraltar. The tremendous strategic importance of Gibraltar is summed up in this view of the relatively narrow passage from the Atlantic to the Mediterranean. To the right, in the distance, is Tarifa (Spain) and to the left, the point north of Tangier (Morocco). (Author's photo)

a fine and very large bay. It is the famous Rock of Gibraltar, a formidable natural fortress. It covers nearly the whole length of the peninsula, its most commanding part forming its northern boundary with, just further north, the flat, narrow and sandy causeway now called the Neutral Grounds leading into the Spanish mainland. The Rock itself decreases more or less gradually until it reaches the southern toe of the peninsula called Europa Point. Its western face is a lofty cliff, which becomes flatter as one descends it, tier after tier, until the seashore is reached. The eastern side, however, forms an extremely abrupt precipice down into the sea. The Rock is of limestone and honeycombed with caves.

The Rock was the Pillars of Hercules of the ancient Greeks as it marked the mythical god's conquests and the western boundary of their world. Phoenician mariners sailed past it going as far as Britain. Carthaginians and Romans battled in its area two centuries before the birth of Christ and, in 171 BC, the vicinity of Gibraltar – then called Carteia – was home to some 4,000 souls, the offspring of Roman legionnaires and Iberian women. Carteia was gradually abandoned after the end of the civil wars and the establishment of the Roman Empire. Under the 'Pax Romana', the strategic importance of the Rock dwindled considerably in a unified Roman world.

The collapse of the Western Roman Empire in the fifth century AD brought about a partition of Western Europe by the various invading hordes of barbarians. The Iberian peninsula basically became the domain of the Goths who, in time, became Christians. In North Africa, the post-Roman world there was swept by the rise of Islam during the seventh century. Gibraltar was to quickly regain its prime strategic importance as two worlds, Islamic North Africa and Christian Europe, collided.

In 711 AD, the great Muslim armies under Tarik-ibn-Zeyad that invaded the southern parts of Western Europe came from North Africa through Gibraltar. Indeed, it is said that the name Gibraltar is a deformation of 'Jebel-Tarik', meaning Tarik's Hill. The Christians, under Roderick, the 'last of the Goths', were overrun by the Arab invaders and most of Spain became a Muslim enclave. But the Christians fought back to reconquer the lost lands in a struggle, the 'Reconquista', that would last nearly eight centuries. In 1160, the Caliph of Morocco, Abd-al-Munnin, ordered that a fortified city be built on the western side of the Rock, where the present town of Gibraltar is situated, and sent architects, engineers, artisans, workers and settlers to the site. Soon, a lovely city with domes, minarets, fountains, strong walls and a castle thrived.

But this was the era of the Christians' steady and implacable re-conquest of the Muslim kingdoms in the Iberian peninsula. During the Middle Ages, Gibraltar was taken and re-taken time and again by successive waves of Muslim and Christian armies. It was not until 1462 that the Spanish crusaders finally prevailed in the possession of Gibraltar. Thirty years later, the last Muslim kingdom in Spain vanished with the capture of Grenada by the armies of Fernando of Aragon and Isabella of Castile, giving birth to a Spanish united kingdom. Gibraltar suffered some disturbances thereafter, notably at the hand of Algerian pirates, but the building of new walls to protect the town and its small harbour, in the middle of the 16th century, gave the place a century-and-a-half of peace and quiet.

A Gibraltar monkey or Rock Ape. The Rock is the only place in Europe that has monkeys running wild. They seemingly were introduced from Morocco as pets in the 18th century. Some obviously got away and made unreachable parts of the Rock their home. There is a legend affirming that if the monkeys vanish from Gibraltar, British rule will end. During the Second World War, a tense period for Gibraltar, the monkey population was said to be down to only four and Prime Minister Winston Churchill made well-publicized arrangements for a reinforcement of monkeys from Morocco! (Author's photo)

A view of the town of Gibraltar from the end of the Old Mole. The old walls and the castle put up by the Moors in the Middle Ages that face Spain on the north side can be clearly seen in this 19th-century rendering. The castle (at top) was built in the 1330s. The Moorish fortifications were kept in good repair and, perched on a steep cliff, still made a formidable obstacle at the time of the Great Siege. Part of the shore batteries that protected the Waterport are at right. (Author's photo)

ORIGINS OF THE CAMPAIGN

By the early 18th century much had changed in the world. Spain had lost its pre-eminent status as a world superpower in the course of the previous century. Even its crown had become unstable and, as a dynastic crisis emerged in 1700 following the death of King Carlos II, a contest developed between Louis XIV's France, the greatest continental power in Europe, and a coalition of countries led by Austria, Britain and Holland, both of the latter being primarily naval rather than continental powers. Louis XIV had chosen his grandson Philip to be king of Spain, as Felipe V, while the allies favoured Charles, of the royal house of Hapsburg, as Carlos III. At stake lay the control of Spain's important holdings in Europe as well as its enormous and fabled colonial empire. Thus did Europe become engulfed in the War of Spanish Succession from 1702, often called Queen Anne's War by North Americans.

For Britain the war presented an opportunity to expand its growing naval power into an area it had never ventured into before – the Mediterranean. This large inland sea was the trade route of incredible wealth between the great Christian nations to the north, namely France, Spain and the Italian states, and the Muslim domains to the south and to the east, namely the Turkish Empire, Egypt and Arab North Africa extending to the Atlantic. The predominant Christian powers had vanquished the Turks and Arabs at Lepanto in 1571 for naval control of the Mediterranean as far east as the Balkans and the situation had since remained much the same. The Mediterranean naval squadrons of France and Spain, the more powerful Italian states such as Venice and Genoa, and the ships of the Order of Malta controlled most of the sea. The only constant challenge came from the redoubtable Arab pirates based on the hostile Barbary Coast – present-day Morocco, Algeria, Tunisia and Libya. On the shores of the Mediterranean Sea stood some of the world's great trading and political centres – Istanbul, Rome, Alexandria, Athens, Beirut, Naples, Algiers, Venice, Barcelona and Marseilles. British traders had ventured in the Mediterranean where they had been, at best, tolerated as novelties. As the war got under way in 1702, all this was about to change.

'...whoever commands the ocean, commands the trade of the world, and whoever commands the trade of the world, commands the riches of the world, and whoever is master of that, commands the world itself.' So wrote John Evelyn in his 1674 *Navigation and Commerce*, which neatly summed up Britain's strategic ambitions.

Looking at a map, the British quickly saw that, as the Mediterranean only had the narrow Straits of Gibraltar to access the Atlantic Ocean and all the world's oceans, whoever controlled the Straits had a definite advantage. And if the country controlling the Straits was a substantial naval power, that

The Southport Gate. Built in 1552, the coat of arms that features the double-headed eagle of Spain's Hapsburg rulers can still be seen above the gateway. (Author's photo)

would give it a tremendous commercial and military geostrategic advantage. Given sufficient naval resources, that country would oversee the naval traffic in and out of the Mediterranean and gain substantial influence and wealth in that area. Spain held Gibraltar in Europe as well as Ceuta in Morocco so its control of the Straits certainly seemed quite solid. But, with the War of Spanish Succession getting under way, Spain's rivals noted that a vital element was missing from the equation: Spain's naval power had practically vanished. With British troops in Portugal moving by land into Spain with their Portuguese and Dutch allies, Britain was now ready to position a powerful squadron off the coast of southern Spain.

France had naturally come to the same conclusion and certainly did not wish to have the British or their allies anywhere near the Straits. In this respect, most Spaniards agreed with the French and they generally supported Louis XIVs Gallic grandson to be their ruler as Felipe V over the rather Germanic Carlos III, who seemed to be too well supported by Spain's ancient and bitter enemies to be acceptable. Thus, by the end of 1703, the great majority of the Spanish armed forces on land and sea and overseas had declared for Felipe V. Nevertheless, by then, British, Dutch and Portuguese troops were in Spain, hoping to gather support for Carlos.

GIBRALTAR FALLS TO BRITAIN

In May 1704, a combined British and Dutch squadron under the command of Admiral Sir George Rooke ventured into the western Mediterranean. On 17 July, Rooke held a council of war with his senior officers to determine what the fleet should do and it was then decided to attack Gibraltar. It was a strong position but might fall if attacked swiftly. On 21 July, the Anglo-Dutch fleet arrived in the bay of Gibraltar and landed some 1,800 British and Dutch troops, led by the Prince of Hesse-Darmstadt, on the isthmus just north of the Rock (now called the Neutral Grounds). This cut off the fortress from mainland Spain. Apart from the 150 men making up the rather meagre garrison of Gibraltar, the Spanish did not have any substantial body of troops in the area and certainly no squadron capable of challenging Rooke's powerful fleet. The Marquis de Salines and his small garrison were trapped but declined Rooke's invitation to capitulate the stronghold to the service of Carlos III. They proclaimed to be true and loyal subjects of their rightful king, Felipe V, and replied they would not give up the place without a fight.

While Gibraltar did not have at that time the maze of fortifications for which it was later to become renowned, it was nevertheless quite a strong position armed with about 100 guns. To the Anglo-Dutch force, a heavy bombardment was the order of the day and, early on 23 July, Sir George Rooke ordered 15 British and six Dutch men-of-war to move up and fire on Gibraltar's defences. They poured a withering fire on the harbour's fortifications, the ships shooting some 15,000 rounds at them in the next five or six hours, sometimes at near-point-blank range. The Spanish gunners did all they could and served their guns admirably but were eventually driven from their positions. The second stage of the attack came as the Allied ships' longboats, full of sailors and troops, made for the Old Mole head. The landing was made with great speed and met with relatively feeble opposition from the few Spanish troops that were

rapidly withdrawing from the Old Mole's fortifications towards the town. There was good reason for their haste: unbeknown to the British and Dutch, the Spanish had prepared a powerful mine to check the assault they had expected. As hundreds of British troops and sailors rushed in, the Spanish sprang the mine that blew up the Old Mole's fortifications in a tremendous explosion. Two lieutenants and 40 men were killed with another 60 wounded by the blast but the survivors on the Old Mole did not panic and held the position as even more troops and sailors were landed from the warships.

With the landing site secured, the fresh troops attacked and took a small redoubt half way between the Old Mole and the town. Not much more stood in the allies' way if they wished to storm the town. In the code of warfare in practice amongst European nations at the time, there was concern not to unduly expose defenceless civilians to the horrors of an assault, which could mean murder, rape and pillage by battle-crazed soldiers. Adm Rooke therefore renewed his call for capitulation and the marquis, having certainly put up an honourable defence in the face of overwhelming odds, and wishing to spare the civilians further harm, surrendered with the 'honours of war'. The next day, 24 July 1704, the remnants of the Spanish garrison marched out towards Spain with its colours flying, drums beating and soldiers bearing their weapons. Those inhabitants that chose to leave could do so with their belongings; those that stayed were guaranteed the same rights as Spaniards as they had enjoyed under King Carlos II. The losses to the attacking force had been high, with two officers and 57 men killed, and eight officers and 217 men wounded. All the same, this famous fortress had fallen to the allies. The Prince of Hesse-Darmstadt was named governor and was left at Gibraltar with as many troops as could be spared. The prince immediately asked for reinforcements for 'the preservation of this important place' of whatever infantry that could be sent with 200 gunners, 'six very good mortar pieces and two hundred iron guns, all of the biggest sizes' (WO 55/343).

Sir George Rooke sailed out as soon as he could. He had intelligence that a French fleet had sailed from Toulon, in southern France, and he went to look for it. Sure enough, the High Admiral of France, the Comte

Gibraltar at about 1700. This contemporary Spanish model of the Rock is not to scale and exaggerates various features and structures, but it does give an idea of the type of fortifications the British and the Dutch faced when they attacked in 1704. While looking impressive, the defences were somewhat medieval in style and thus outdated. (Museo Naval, Madrid. Author's photo)

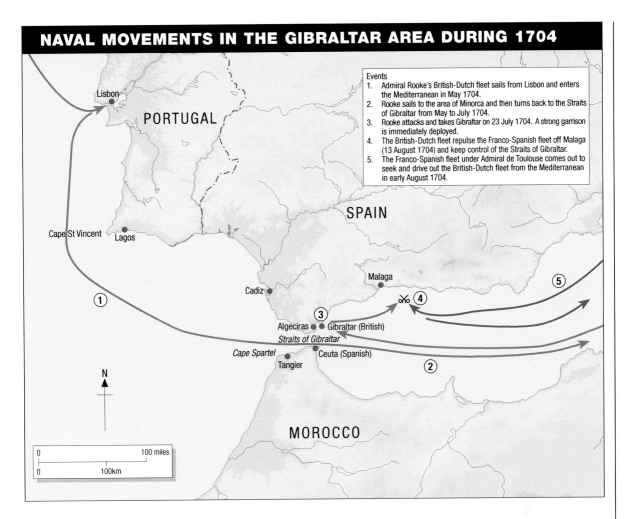

NAVAL MOVEMENTS IN THE GIBRALTAR AREA DURING 1704

Lisbon

PORTUGAL

SPAIN

Cape St Vincent

Lagos

Malaga

Cadiz

Algeciras

Gibraltar (British)

Straits of Gibraltar

Cape Spartel

Ceuta (Spanish)

Tangier

MOROCCO

N

| 0 | 100 miles |
| 0 | 100km |

Events

1. Admiral Rooke's British-Dutch fleet sails from Lisbon and enters the Mediterranean in May 1704.
2. Rooke sails to the area of Minorca and then turns back to the Straits of Gibraltar from May to July 1704.
3. Rooke attacks and takes Gibraltar on 23 July 1704. A strong garrison is immediately deployed.
4. The British-Dutch fleet repulse the Franco-Spanish fleet off Malaga (13 August 1704) and keep control of the Straits of Gibraltar.
5. The Franco-Spanish fleet under Admiral de Toulouse comes out to seek and drive out the British-Dutch fleet from the Mediterranean in early August 1704.

British and Dutch troops in longboats about to land at Gibraltar on 23 July 1704. (Plate from Cannon's *History of the 4th Regiment of Foot*. Author's photo)

de Toulouse, was leading a large fleet towards southern Spain. The news of a large Anglo-Dutch fleet lurking about the western Mediterranean certainly upset the French and they were determined to drive out the intruders. Most of his warships were French with a few Spanish men-o'-war and galleys added.

On 13 August 1704, Rooke's Anglo-Dutch fleet sighted de Toulouse's Franco-Spanish fleet off Malaga. Rooke had the numerical advantage, with 41 English and 12 Dutch ships-of-the-line, six frigates and seven fireships, while de Toulouse had 50 ships-of-the-line, eight frigates, nine fireships and 25 oared galleys. The Franco-Spanish fleet had three ships of 104 guns each and four with 90 to 92 guns, while the largest ships of the Anglo-Dutch fleet were three men-of-war of 96 guns, so that the latter's numerical advantage was somewhat tempered by this. Battle lines were formed and both fleets fired broadsides at each other all day. Although the engagement was very sharp and hotly contested, there was no clear winner by the evening when both fleets broke off. All the ships engaged had been damaged and each side had several thousand sailors killed and wounded. Both Rooke and de Toulouse claimed to be winners and solemn special religious services celebrating the victory were eventually held at St Paul's in London and at Notre-Dame in Paris. Admiral de Toulouse returned to Toulon with his battered fleet while the control of the straits of Gibraltar remained with the Anglo-Dutch allies.

When the news of Gibraltar's fall reached Madrid, the Spanish court of Felipe V was very upset as it fully understood the strategic implications of its loss. The Marquis de Villadaria was ordered to march south at the head of 8,000 troops with instructions to re-take Gibraltar. Hearing of this, the Earl of Galway, commander-in-chief of allied forces in Portugal, sent reinforcements from Lisbon, consisting of four regiments with supplies and ammunition to Gibraltar, by now surrounded by Villadaria's army. On 27 October, the troops and supplies arrived at the Rock on board Sir John Leake's fleet. The besieging Spanish sensed that they needed to attack right away before more reinforcements to the garrison arrived by sea. Bombardments alone could not do it. A frontal assault by land was possible but ruled out as near suicidal. However, a sort of 'commando' party might succeed and that plan was blessed. Some 500 volunteers stepped up, resolved to take and hold the gates long enough for their comrades, massed just beyond the Neutral Grounds, to rush in and take the place by storm. They sneaked up to the Rock's heights and actually slept in St George's Cave on 31 October without being detected. The next day, they overpowered the British guards at the Signal-House and at Middle Hill but were spotted by British sentinels who gave the alarm. Before long, British battalions marched up and charged the out-numbered Spaniards who retreated back towards the top of the cliff. About a hundred were killed by bayonet or hurled over the precipice while a colonel and about 30 men surrendered, the rest presumably making their escape. The Spanish 'commando' attempt had utterly failed.

The Marquis of Villadaria was not discouraged by the raid's failure and maintained the pressure on Gibraltar's garrison. A constant bombardment was kept up on the defences and two breaches were made in the ramparts facing the Neutral Grounds. Having received substantial reinforcements, Villadaria resolved to storm one of the breaches. The Spanish 'Forlorn Hope' was initially successful but the sound of fighting at the breach gave the alarm to the rest of the garrison in town. Its regiments mustered and drove out the attackers.

The failure of the attack led to the replacement of the Marquis de Villadaria by Marshal de Tessé, a veteran French commander. The Spanish entrenchments were improved and additional guns mounted to bombard Gibraltar. The Spanish and French were fully aware that the garrison was holding out thanks to supplies and reinforcements that came by sea. Admiral de Pointis was to blockade Gibraltar with a powerful Franco-Spanish squadron. The British took the menace very seriously because the Rock was bound to fall should it succeed. Admiral Sir John Leake's Royal Naval squadron at Lisbon accordingly sailed towards Gibraltar and, on 10 March 1705, caught up with de Pointis who was utterly defeated, losing five ships. On the shore, Marshal de Tessé could only watch the Franco-Spanish naval defeat in despair as he knew that, without naval control, Gibraltar could not be taken. A tight blockade on land was maintained but no further attempts were made during the War of the Spanish Succession.

In 1713, the Treaty of Utrecht recognized Felipe V as the legitimate king of Spain but it also ceded Gibraltar and Minorca, which had also been captured in 1708, to Great Britain. It stated that the King of Spain 'does hereby, for himself, his heirs, and successors, yield to the Crown of Great Britain the full and entire property of the town and castle of Gibraltar, together with the port, fortifications, and forts thereunto belonging; and he gives up the said property to be held and enjoyed absolutely with all manner of right for ever, without any exception or impediment whatsoever'.

In the event, Britain suddenly had virtual control over the entrance of the Mediterranean thanks to Gibraltar and a powerful base in the western

part of that sea by its possession of Minorca. For Spain and France, this presented a wholly new and very uncomfortable geostrategic equation.

The ink was hardly dry on the treaty before King Felipe was trying every trick in the book to regain the Rock in times of war or peace and this has been continued by 'his heirs, and successors' to this day. The Spanish always hoped that the next war would provide the opportunity to re-take Gibraltar.

In 1720, Britain and Spain were at war and the Spanish planned a surprise attack. A large body of Spanish troops and ships under the command of the Marquis de Leda was gathered at Gibraltar Bay, supposedly to reinforce Spain's African enclave at Ceuta. The real object, according to British spies, was to mount a surprise attack on Gibraltar. The Rock's garrison was then quite weak, consisting of only three infantry battalions with some gunners. But Britain had naval superiority and used it to advantage. The Spanish surprise was foiled when part of Minorca's garrison was conveyed by the Royal Navy to reinforce Gibraltar. All Spanish hopes to take the Rock thus vanished and the Marquis de Leda did sail for Ceuta with his troops after all.

A few more years of peace went by until February 1727 when hostilities again erupted between Spain and Britain. Naturally, re-taking Gibraltar was high on the Spanish agenda and a substantial army under the Count de Los Torres gathered and started to build batteries on the Neutral Grounds. They were soon driven off, however, by the British guns. The Spanish then started digging a mine intended to make a breach in the walls but the scheme was discovered and countered by British engineers. Artillery duels followed without much effect on either side. In late April, word came that the war had ended and the siege was raised.

The 90-gun HMS *Prince George* battering Spanish ships at the naval battle off Malaga on 13 August 1704. Adm Sir George Rooke's Anglo-Dutch fleet's victory over the French and Spanish fleet secured Gibraltar to the British and, for the first time, brought in a powerful British naval presence in the western Mediterranean that would last some three centuries. (Print after Charles Dixon. Author's photo)

Gibraltar thus remained a possession of Great Britain. For the next 52 years, Spain made no further attempt to retake the place although there were hostilities against Britain in 1739–48 and 1762–63.

MINORCA

The military history of Gibraltar in the 18th century is inseparable from that of the other British outpost in the Mediterranean, the island of Minorca. On 14 September 1708, an Anglo-Dutch naval squadron landed a force on the island, which was claimed in the name of the Austrian pretender to the Spanish crown. The island's population greeted the British and Dutch soldiers as liberators. A week later, the Franco-Spanish garrison favouring the French pretender surrendered. The British posted a strong garrison to the island. By the terms of the 1713 Treaty of Utrecht, Minorca was ceded to Great Britain.

The permanent presence of the British at Minorca was deeply disturbing to Spain and France. This relatively small island of 45km from east to west by 17km at its widest point was considered a great danger as it could be used by the Royal Navy to raid the Spanish and French Mediterranean coast. The British were very aware of this advantage and, over the next decades, greatly improved the island's fortifications, especially Fort St Philip at the town of Mahon, which became a powerful citadel, largely through the efforts of Governor Richard Kane. He also had a road built that crossed the island and he took care to respect the Catholic faith of the islanders. As a result, the island's economy flourished and the Minorcans were pleased with British rule.

The French, however, were far from pleased with a British presence that threatened their ports of Marseilles and Toulon. In April 1756, shortly after the declaration of war, a French fleet appeared, outwitted Admiral Byng's Royal Naval squadron and landed some 12,000 troops on the island under the command of Marshal de Richelieu. The isolated and heavily outnumbered British garrison surrendered on 10 July after a siege of two months. Britons were outraged at the loss and Admiral Byng was court-martialled and executed as a result, '*pour encourager les autres*' (to encourage the others), as the French philosopher Voltaire put it. Minorca remained in French hands for seven years but was returned to Great Britain by the Treaty of Paris in 1763.

The next period of British rule was not as popular with Minorcans as previously. Trade and commerce did not flourish as before, restrictions were brought against the Catholic Church and British officials were suspected of lining their pockets. Most of the island's 27,000 souls took a 'wait and see' stance. From 1774, General James Murray was governor and his style of government was not especially popular amongst the native Minorcans. When war was declared, he distributed some 50 *lettres de marque* to corsairs and was believed to have cashed in a percentage of the profits. Meanwhile, in Madrid, Prime Minister Floridablanca was taking steps to prepare a campaign to retake Minorca, as was wished by King Carlos III. The French also wanted the British out of Minorca and were prepared to provide ships and troops that would join the Spanish forces to achieve this objective.

CHRONOLOGY

711

Muslim army crosses from Africa to Spain; tradition has it that it landed in Gibraltar.

1090

Spanish Christian army reconquers southern Spain.

1146

Gen Abd al-Mumin invades southern Spain leading a Muslim army from Morocco through Tarifa, gains control of much of the country including Gibraltar.

1160

Gen Abd al-Mumin decrees the building of fortifications at Gibraltar.

1309

Gibraltar besieged and captured by Spanish.

1315

Moors' siege to recapture Gibraltar fails.

1333

Moors besiege and capture Gibraltar in June.

1349–50

King Alfonso XI of Castile lays siege to Gibraltar but the 'Black Death' ravages the Spanish army and the siege is given up after Alfonso's death in March 1350.

1436

Spanish troops fail to retake Gibraltar from Moors.

1462

Spanish troops capture Gibraltar. The town is given a charter by King Henry IV of Castile.

1466–67

Duke of Medina Sidonia's forces besieges rival forces of Governor Villacreces in Gibraltar who finally surrenders after 15 months.

1492

The kingdom of Grenada, last Muslim stronghold in the peninsula, falls to the Spanish forces; Christopher Columbus discovers America.

1506

Duke of Medina Sidonia's rebel forces besiege royal forces in Gibraltar but fail to capture it.

1540

September Algerian pirates raid and loot the town of Gibraltar but fail to overcome the garrison in the castle.

1550s

Walls built to enclose the town by order of Emperor Charles V.

1702

Outbreak of the War of Spanish Succession.

1704

23 July British and Dutch forces attack Gibraltar, Spanish garrison capitulates and formally surrenders with the Honours of War the next day.
13 August Anglo-Dutch fleet repulse Franco-Spanish fleet off Malaga and keep control of the Straits of Gibraltar.
November Spanish besiege Gibraltar; an assault to retake it is repulsed.

1705

7 February French and Spanish assault on Gibraltar fails, siege lifted in April.

1708

British capture Minorca.

1713

Gibraltar and Minorca formally ceded to Great Britain by the peace Treaty of Utrecht.

1727

Spanish army begins siege operations in February. After heavy bombardments that proved ineffective, the siege is lifted in April.

1756

Seven Years' War breaks out; French capture Minorca in 1756, which is returned to Britain in 1763 by the Treaty of Paris.

1769–79

Major improvements to the fortifications of Gibraltar are carried out under the direction of Chief Engineer William Green.

1772

Soldier Artificers Company raised.

1775

Outbreak of the American War of Independence.

1776

MajGen George Augustus Eliott appointed governor of Gibraltar.

1778

France becomes the ally of the Americans and enters the war against Britain.

1779

21 June Spain having declared war to Britain, communications are cut with Gibraltar and the Great Siege starts.

1780

25 January Adm Rodney's fleet arrives in Gibraltar, lands 73rd Highland Regiment and supplies.
7 June Spanish fireship attack fails.

1781

12 April Adm Darby arrives in Gibraltar with a relief fleet of over 100 ships,.
27 November British and Hanoverian troops make a daring and successful sortie on the Spanish lines.

1782

5 February Fort St Philip at Port Mahon, Minorca, capitulates to the Spanish and French after an heroic resistance of nearly six months by Gen Murray and his garrison.
21–22 March British ships bring supplies and the sickly 97th Regiment to Gibraltar.
June Work on tunnel begun by SgtMaj Ince and his artificers.
June French troops join the Spanish. The Duc de Crillon assumes overall command of the siege operations against Gibraltar.
13 September Attack of the floating batteries fails, all being destroyed by Gibraltar's defenders.
18 October Adm Howe's relief fleet arrives and lands the 25th and 59th regiments to reinforce Gibraltar's garrison.

1783

3 February Fighting ends and the blockade is lifted after the Duc de Crillon advises Governor Eliott that peace has been signed at Versailles on 20 January; end of the Great Siege.
12 March Gates of Gibraltar open.
September Minorca ceded to Spain and Gibraltar remains British by the Treaty of Versailles.

1941

Most of the civilian population is evacuated to Morocco, Madeira, Jamaica and Britain, repatriated in 1945; permanent Royal Air Force airfield begun in October 1941, completed in July 1943.

1968

6 May Spanish government closes the frontier of Gibraltar.

1985

5 February Border with Spain is reopened after a 16-year blockade.

OPPOSING COMMANDERS

BRITISH COMMANDERS

Lieutenant-General George Augustus Eliott (1717–90), the 'hero of Gibraltar' and 'Cock of the Rock', was the seventh son of the Baronet of Stobs in Roxburghshire, Scotland. Educated at the University of Leyden in Holland and at the French military academy of La Fère, he joined the British army aged 17 and served both in the Horse Grenadier Guards and as a field engineer. In the 1740s, he campaigned in Flanders and King George II made him his ADC in 1756. In 1759, he encouraged new tactics and raised the 15th Light Dragoons, one of the new light cavalry regiments. He was also promoted to major-general that year and, in 1762, was second-in-command to Lord Albermarle at the siege and capture of Havana, the prize money of which made him a wealthy lieutenant-general.

The post-war period was somewhat quiet and, in 1774, now a widower, he accepted the role of commander-in-chief in Ireland but soon asked to be recalled. His next posting, in 1777, perfectly suited his character – the governorship of Gibraltar. Eliott was a stern person with austere manners; he only drank water and was a vegetarian. Indeed, during the Great Siege, he refused all privileges regarding food and this had an immense effect on the garrison's good morale. He was a disciplinarian and had many soldiers executed for desertion, robbery and drunkenness. Still, he was seen as being fair. He was rarely regarded with either warmth or affection, but commanded considerable respect.

When Eliott arrived, he found the Rock in good condition largely thanks to LtCol William Green of the engineers who had improved the fortifications. Soon after Eliott's arrival, the rumours of war with Spain grew, even more so after France entered the conflict in June 1778. A year later, Spain declared war. Thanks to the resolute attitude of its governor, who seemed to embody all the virtues of steadfast resistance and defiance against the odds, the spirits of the men defending Gibraltar were kept high right up to the end of the Great Siege. The conduct of the garrison and its commander won the admiration of friends and foes. Eliott, as dour as ever, was thanked by Parliament, knighted in 1783, and in 1787 raised to the peerage as Lord Heathfield, Baron of Gibraltar. On 6 July 1790 while at Aix-la-Chapelle, this outstanding soldier died of palsy in his 73rd year.

Lieutenant-General Robert Boyd (1710–94) was lieutenant-governor of Gibraltar during the Great Siege. Originally he was a civil official in the Board of Ordnance who had distinguished himself at the 1756 siege of Minorca and at the battle of Minden three years later. Much appreciated in high circles, he became colonel of the 39th Foot, major-general and lieutenant-governor of Gibraltar, a place that he greatly appreciated.

George Augustus Eliott, Lord Heathfield and Baron of Gibraltar, c. 1790, aptly nicknamed 'The Cock of the Rock' for his stubborn defence. He was elevated to the peerage in 1787 and wears the uniform of a full general, as can be seen by the evenly spaced embroidered buttonholes, a rank he achieved after the Great Siege. The burning Spanish ships are shown on the lower left background. (Print after Pozzi. Author's photo)

The British and Hanoverian officers at the Great Siege. From left to right, main centre group: Lt Governor Sir Robert Boyd; MajGen De la Motte; Governor Eliott (mounted); Chief Engineer Sir William Green; Col Dachenhausen of Reden's Regt; MajGen Picton; Col Schleppegrell of De la Motte's Regt; Col Hugo (looking back) of Hardenberg's Regt; LtCol Vaughan, 39th Foot; Col Trigge, 12th Foot; Col Craig, 56th Foot; LtCol Hardy, Quartermaster General; LtCol Lindsay, 73rd Foot (in Highland dress); Maj Brown, 58th Foot. Group above: Maj Perryn, 12th Foot; Lt Holloway, ADC to Chief Engineer; Capt Drinkwater, 72nd Foot and author of the best-known history of the siege. Below: Maj Vallotton, first ADC to the Governor (holding a telescope); Col Lewis commanding the artillery. The colouring of the uniforms in this print is occasionally erroneous; for instance the 73rd had buff facings and silver lace. (Detail from a print after J.S. Copley's *The Defeat of the Floating Batteries at Gibraltar*. Anne S.K. Brown Military Collection, Brown University, Providence, USA. Author's photo)

Disappointed at not obtaining the Rock's governorship in 1777, he was rather cool to Governor Eliott but, in spite of being sickly, General Boyd was an able second-in-command during the Great Siege. He finally succeeded Lord Heathfield as governor of Gibraltar and passed away at the Rock.

The credit for Gibraltar's conservation also goes to **Lieutenant-Colonel William Green** of the Royal Engineers. An Irishman educated at Woolwich, Green had campaigned in Europe and North America. Wounded at Quebec in 1759, he was promoted lieutenant-colonel and named chief engineer at Gibraltar, a task he took to heart. What he found there was cause for concern and, in 1769, he gave evidence on the defects in the Rock's fortifications to the parliamentary commission of enquiry held at Westminster. The following years were spent supervising constructions, notably the King's Bastion that was to be so important in Gibraltar's defence. He also organized the Company of Artificers in 1772.

Many other officers in the garrison behaved superbly during the Great Siege. The officers of the Hanoverian contingent were outstanding, as were their men. The officers of the Royal Artillery, were tireless in countless artillery duels. **Lieutenant Koelher** stands out among them for his innovative inventions.

Captain Leslie initially commanded the naval forces at Gibraltar. **Captain Sir Roger Curtis** replaced him in April 1781 and remained until the end of the siege. He was an energetic young commander who was well liked and drew the praise of the old governor for his daring actions. He was made a brigadier when the Marine Brigade was formed in late August 1782. He went back carrying dispatches to England with Lord Howe's fleet in November 1782, coming back with the thanks of the king and Parliament in March 1783.

FRANCO-SPANISH COMMANDERS

Louis de Balbe de Berton, Duc de Crillon and Marshal of France, commanded the Spanish and French land forces that took the island of Minorca from the British in February 1782. He was then appointed to command the Hispano-French forces at the siege operations aimed at taking Gibraltar. (Print after portrait. Author's photo)

Jean-Claude-Éléonor Le Michaud, Chevalier D'Arçon of the French Corps of Engineers, came up with the concept of using floating batteries to breach Gibraltar's harbour defences. Had the attack of September 1782 been carried out as he had planned, it might have succeeded. (Print after a 1790s profile portrait. Author's photo)

Louis de Balbe de Berton, Duc de Crillon (1717–96), took over command of the Franco-Spanish forces besieging Gibraltar in 1782 in his 65th year. His arrival heralded the most intense period of the Great Siege. By his own account, he had been present at 68 actions and 22 sieges so he was an experienced soldier. Born into the high nobility, his military career began in 1731 as a cadet in the royal guard. Commissioned two years later, he rose to colonel of the Bretagne Infantry Regiment in 1738 and went on to become major-general campaigning in Italy during the War of the Austrian Succession. Possessing administrative talents and great charm, he was named governor-general of the province of Picardie after the war, going back into the armed forces during the Seven Years' War, and was wounded at Rossbach. He certainly did not rule out original ideas and, in 1758, actively promoted the concept of invading England by an amphibious operation that would have transported a large French army across the Channel. His proposal was not acted upon by the French court, but it had the merit of being the only real threat made against Britain, which mobilized its militia and home fleet as a result. His association with Spain started with his involvement in the Spanish attempt to invade Portugal in 1762. He stayed with the Spanish Army's staff after the war and, in 1765, was put in command of the 'Campo de Gibraltar' as the usually small Spanish force posted near the Rock was called. He later went on to other functions and, in 1781, took command of the Franco-Spanish expedition to take Minorca. Following the surrender of the island, de Crillon was made Duc de Mahon and a Spanish Grandee by a delighted Carlos III.

Appointed to command the forces at Gibraltar, de Crillon assumed the post without too many illusions. An experienced siege commander, he grasped what a formidable challenge the Rock presented and, while he hoped the floating-batteries scheme might work, he did not entertain great confidence in the whole operation. Too many elements might go wrong and his foreboding proved to be correct. The siege's failure destroyed his reputation and his subsequent disputes with D'Arçon made him pass for a bitter old man.

Jean-Claude-Éléonor Le Michaud, Chevalier D'Arçon (1733–1800), was a bright French engineer officer who had been noted at the defence of Cassel in 1761. He went up the ranks and was colonel in 1782 when sent to Gibraltar. His concept of the floating batteries certainly had merit, given the technology of the time, and presented the only really serious threat made to the Rock during the Great Siege. The batteries' failure did not disgrace him and he went on to become general and inspector of fortifications. He served in the field with French armies in 1791–93 and was made senator the year before his death.

Of the Spanish commanders, **Vice-Admiral Antonio de Barcelo** (1717–97) was the most notable. A native of Palma de Mallorca, Barcelo was a tough and unsophisticated sailor who came up through the ranks by his relentless and successful actions against the Algerian pirates that infested the Spanish coast. He was not a nobleman and it was said that he could hardly sign his name. He had few friends but was very popular with lower-deck seamen and, in spite of his rough manners, appreciated by King Carlos III. Considered an excellent 'corsair', his lack of formal education prevented his appointment as senior fleet commander. During the Great Siege his light craft and gunboats were probably the most effective and annoying naval prods against the Rock. However, his bitterness at being superseded by Admiral de Cordova in 1782 may have had negative effects on the main attack during the Great Siege.

Little seems known of **Rear-Admiral Bonaventura Moreno** whose naval squadron did not seal Minorca too well during its siege and who commanded with great bravery the doomed floating batteries. He was certainly not found to be very effective in the opinion of his French allies. Nor was **Admiral Luis de Cordova**, Spain's senior sailor, who always seemed to avoid action and whose large squadrons were unable to block and outwit the British fleets sent to supply Gibraltar.

Army generals commanding the Spanish forces do not appear to have displayed outstanding qualities or much vigour during the Great Siege. The undefended state of the forward lines that Governor Eliott found in his November 1781 sortie does not point to remarkable leadership from the Spanish commanders.

V Adm Antonio de Barcelo commanded the Spanish warships that blockaded Gibraltar for most of the siege. An experienced sailor, he tended to rely on small and fast-moving gunboats to hinder Gibraltar's communications and supplies. He was probably the most talented of the Spanish commanders at the siege. (Museo Naval, Madrid. Author's photo)

OPPOSING ARMIES

THE BRITISH GARRISON

At the time of Spain's declaration of war, in June 1779, the British garrison of Gibraltar amounted to 5,382 officers and men of all ranks. In spite of losses in action or due to sickness, this number actually increased during the Great Siege due to the arrival of reinforcements and stood at some 7,000 officers and other ranks in 1783.

Once hostilities were declared, Governor Eliott quickly made changes to Gibraltar's command structure, which was temporarily expanded by the local appointment of extra staff. On 25 June 1779, MajGen de la Motte was appointed to that rank on the British staff. He was assisted by an aide-de-camp and a major of brigade. A Quartermaster General, an Adjutant-General and a Director of Hospitals were also appointed at that date. On 17 April 1781, colonels Ross, Green and Picton were given the local rank of brigadier-general, each with the assistance of a major of brigade, as was Colonel Stanton on 5 April 1782. This command structure proved quite effective during the siege.

The infantry from Great Britain in garrison initially consisted of five regiments. At that time, the vast majority of British regiments had only one battalion of ten companies including the two 'Flank', or elite, light infantry and grenadier companies. Their establishment was 577 officers

Royal Artillery Lt G.F. Koehler demonstrating to Governor Eliott his invention of a depressing gun carriage suited to Gibraltar's abrupt cliffs. (Print after E. Hobday. Author's photo)

and men but it was not uncommon for regiments to be considerably under strength. In March 1778, each of the five regiments at Gibraltar were short of over 200 men. Recruits to complete the regiments arrived in July 1778 . Governor Eliott thought they were 'very serviceable'; their good performance during the following years of siege is certainly testimony to the ability of the cadres in their regiment to turn them into peerless soldiers. The 12th Foot had arrived in Gibraltar in 1769 and left after the Great Siege. The 39th Foot was posted at the Rock from 1766 and remained in the fortress until the end of the Great Siege. The 56th Foot came to Gibraltar in 1770. The 58th arrived in 1770 and departed in 1784.

From 1778 to 1782, five more British battalions were sent to Gibraltar. The 72nd (Royal Manchester Volunteers) was a new regiment raised from 17 December 1777 and arrived at Gibraltar on 8 July 1778. Governor Eliott thought they were 'a remarkably fine body of men' (CO 91/24). It served there until the end of the siege and was disbanded after the end of the war. The 2nd Battalion of the 73rd (McLeod's Highlanders) was raised in 1778 and its 1,052 men were the first reinforcements to reach Gibraltar in January 1780. The battalion was disbanded following the end of the hostilities. The 97th was raised in 1780 and arrived at Gibraltar on 25 March 1782 as a reinforcement that seemed 'compleat but rather unhealthy' to Governor Eliott. Yet it had already been noted for its gallantry in action at sea against Dutch ships while travelling to the Rock. By June, Eliott could report that its sickly men were 'recovering' and 'all the rest of the garrison were remarkably healthy' (CO 97/28). It was disbanded on its return to Britain after the Great Siege. The 25th was in Minorca from 1769 to 1775, came back in the area as reinforcement to Gibraltar on board Lord Howe's fleet in October 1782 and remained in garrison until 1793. The 59th also arrived in Gibraltar on board Lord Howe's fleet in October 1782 and remained posted there until 1792.

In 1776, five battalions of Hanoverian troops were brought out of Germany to reinforce the British garrisons in Gibraltar and Minorca. It will be recalled that, until 1837, Hanover formed part of the United Kingdom. A Hanoverian infantry battalion had an establishment of 460 officers and men, divided into six companies, including one of grenadiers. The first battalions of Hardenberg's, Reden's and de la Motte's regiments were sent to Gibraltar while the second battalions of Prinz Ernst's and Goldacker's regiments joined Minorca's garrison. All five battalions were found by British inspecting officers to be very good troops, always reported as 'fine' and 'fit for any service'. At Gibraltar, the three battalions were under the command of MajGen de la Motte. During the Great Siege, the Hanoverians proved to be some of the steadiest and most reliable soldiers in Gibraltar.

Early in the Great Siege, on 20 August 1779, Governor Eliott gathered the best shots of the various infantry regiments into a distinct temporary company of marksmen, consisting of two NCOs and 64 men under Lt Burleigh of the 39th Foot. They were likely posted in the area of the barriers to keep Spanish scouts at a respectable distance.

The detachment of Royal Artillery played a vital role in Gibraltar as so much of the defence depended on the artillery's performance. In March 1778, as the clouds of war were gathering, Governor Eliott

Officer, Royal Artillery, c. 1778–83. The coats of the officers and men were to have respectively gold and yellow-laced buttonholes as shown. However, a March 1781 inspection of the three Royal Artillery companies at Minorca mentions that the 'Officer's uniform' was 'Plain blue, lapelled to the waist with scarlet cloth, cross pockets, round cuffs with falling collar of ditto [scarlet], Yellow buttons, plain holes, Embroidered epaulettes with gold fringes, plain white cloath Waistcoat and Breeches, plain Hatts with uniform Swords and sword knots.' (WO 34/176). The painting by Copley shows Col Lewis in a plain coat while Trumbull has Lt Koehler with laced buttonholes. Most likely a case of officer's dress and ordinary duty coats. The enlisted men would have had laced buttonholes. (Plate by R.J. Macdonald. Author's photo)

appealed to London that he only had about 130 NCOs and gunners in the five companies in garrison. His urgent call was heard and, in late July, some 247 'fine' artillerymen arrived at the Rock. By June 1779, there were 25 officers and 460 NCOs and gunners but this was totally inadequate to serve over 550 guns and mortars mounted in Gibraltar's various batteries. With the addition of 18 field guns, 4 howitzers and some 90 dismounted but serviceable cannons and mortars, the Rock could boast a total of 663 serviceable pieces of artillery according to an inventory made in March 1783. Governor Eliott detached 180 infantrymen to learn artillery so as to provide additional gunners. As it was, the gunners were kept very busy and, between September 1779 and February 1783, fired no fewer than 57,163 cannon balls, 129,151 mortar and howitzer shells, 12,681 grapeshot, 926 carcasses and 679 light balls. In all, some 200,600 shots that required 8,000 barrels of powder, to which can be added over 4,700 shots fired from British gunboats. All this averaged an amazing 160 shots per day, bearing in mind that there were weeks when only a few shots and days when hundreds of rounds were fired. The British gunners also came up with several inventions and ingenious adaptations during the Great Siege. The best-known invention is Lt Koelher's depressing carriage but there were others, as related in the text and illustrations of this book.

The Company of Artificers was raised in March 1772 at the suggestion of LtCol Green who needed disciplined military artisans to carry out the improvements to Gibraltar's fortifications. It consisted of enlisted men supervised by Royal Engineer officers. During the siege, the engineering service in Gibraltar was divided into three divisions, which were reinforced by several officers detached from infantry regiments to act as assistant engineers and overseers. The corps proved to be very useful and was augmented from 68 men initially to 122 in 1779 and to 234 by August 1782. It gave outstanding service during the siege setting up and repairing the Rock's fortifications. Its most famous deed was suggested by SgtMaj Henry Ince in May 1782: building a subterranean artillery gallery facing north high up in the Rock; work started in June and, by September, five embrasures had been pierced and some 24pdrs installed. Construction of galleries has gone on ever since and the Rock is now said to be honeycombed with some 30 miles (48km) of tunnels.

The Corsican Corps was a rather unusual reinforcement that arrived from Italy on 25 July 1782. It was made up of five officers, eight NCOs and 68 privates, two drummers and a chaplain that had been sponsored by the British representative in Florence. Captain-Commandant Leonetti and his men were Corsican nationalists who had no great affection for the French. Leonetti himself was a nephew of Pasquale Paoli, the leader of Corsican resistance following the island's annexation to France in 1768. Many of his men had previous military experience, some having escaped Minorca before its fall. They were armed with musket, bayonet and a belt pistol and equipped with two cartridge boxes. The Corsican Corps was posted on Windmill Hill, which was rather out of range, and consequently only suffered an officer wounded. Two men died of sickness and, not surprisingly, none of these patriots deserted to the French and Spanish side. Governor Eliott was very pleased with 'the Corsican Corps, whose behaviour…is not only irreproachable, but meritorious' (CO 91/29). The corps was disbanded following the end of the siege.

The uniforms worn by the garrison during the siege were not always the traditional 'redcoats' often shown in illustrations made after the war. The inspection reports reveal that, by February 1781, the clothing of the 12th and 58th, last approved and issued in 1778–79, was still 'tolerably good'. This was not the case for the 39th and 56th who wore 'linen waistcoats and breeches, the cloth ones being mostly worn out'. All regiments wore black half gaiters 'as is usual in this garrison'. The 72nd was never issued red coats, the only clothing received by its men being white jackets with blue facings and 'white linen waistcoats & long canvas trousers'. The 73rd was a regiment of Highlanders whose uniforms had worn out by March 1781 so the men 'appeared in jackets made of their old plaids' with linen waistcoats and 'long linen trousers'. The officers of the 73rd also had 'plaid jackets, linen waistcoats & long linen trousers to be uniform with the men'. The three Hanoverian battalions of Hardenberg, Reden and de la Motte were all in better condition insofar as their 1779 issue clothing, all of which was still considered as 'very good' in 1781. The Hanoverian officers were all reported 'uniformly dressed' (WO 1/972, WO 7/27 and WO 34/141). The garrison's clothing situation improved following the arrival of the regimental uniforms on board of Lord Howe's relief fleet in October 1782.

Gibraltar also had a few Royal Navy ships consisting of the 60-gun ship-of-the-line *Panther*, the 28-gun frigate *Enterprise* and three small gunboats mounting from 10 to 14 guns each. They were manned by a total of 760 officers and ratings under the command of Captain Harvey during most of the siege. The strength could and did vary over the years, with ships coming in and out. Overall, 300 additional sailors reinforced the Rock. Another feature, from June 1782, was the addition of a dozen small gunboats each armed with one gun. At the end of August 1782, with the attack impending, Captain Curtis agreed with Governor Eliott to bring the sailors ashore and form them into a temporary Marine

RIGHT **Grenadiers, Spanish Guard Regiment (left) and Walloon Guard Regiment (right), 1780. These regiments had several battalions each numbering over 6,000 officers and men that were deployed against Gibraltar. A detachment of the Walloon Guards was in the forward lines when the British made their successful sortie on 27 November 1781. Both guard regiments had an almost identical uniform of blue faced with scarlet, the colours of the royal livery. (Anne S.K. Brown Military Collection, Brown University, Providence, USA. Author's photo)**

FAR RIGHT **Grenadier, Napoles Regiment, 1780. Napoles was one of many Spanish line infantry regiments blocking Gibraltar. It wore the typical uniform of Spanish infantry recruited in the country, a white coat with facings of various colours. Napoles had scarlet cuffs, waistcoat and breeches with white metal buttons. The native regiments also wore buff belts rather than white as in guards and foreign regiments. Spanish army grenadiers had fur caps without plates in front but with elaborately decorated bags behind (invisible). (Anne S.K. Brown Military Collection, Brown University, Providence, USA. Author's photo)**

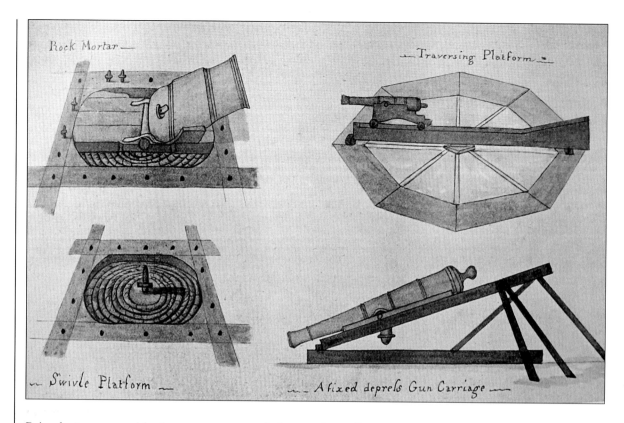

Rock Mortar —

— Traversing Platform —

— Swivle Platform —

— A fixed depreſs Gun Carriage —

Brigade to serve with the army troops of the garrison. It was about 900 strong.

THE SPANISH FORCES

By the time of the American War of Independence, the Spanish Army had been through various reforms since its defeats at the end of the Seven Years' War. Many of these reforms, heralded by King Carlos III, had been influenced by its 18th-century ally: France. The infantry had become well versed in drills and manoeuvres, the officer corps was better educated in the military sciences, the artillery was converting to the state-of-the-art Gribeauval system and the corps of engineers maintained its level of proficiency. This made it a force to be reckoned with and it enjoyed a measure of success in its campaigns against the British in America. Thus, it would seem that a large Spanish army would have a very good chance of overcoming that British thorn in Spain's pride: Gibraltar.

Spain's metropolitan army was organized somewhat along the lines of the French Army since the beginning of the 18th century. It had a large number of guard infantry and cavalry, 42 regiments of line infantry, each having an establishment of 1,446 officers and men divided into two battalions that each had eight fusilier and one grenadier company. There were also four Swiss mercenary infantry regiments, each having 1,462 officers and men, and several other smaller light infantry units. The mounted troops consisted of 22 regiments of dragoons and cavalry; the specialists mustered four battalions of artillery and 150 engineer officers.

Mortars and cannons mounted on various types of platforms put up in Gibraltar during the Great Siege. The gunners made the most of available material with a great deal of imaginative technical innovation. The mortar, for instance, could swivel on its coil rope bed. (Plate from Spillbury's journal. Author's photo)

The metropolitan army's theoretical establishment hovered at about 90,000 officers and men. The army's reserve consisted of 42 regiments of provincial militia of one battalion each whose grenadier companies were often embodied for active service. These grenadier formations were very much like regular troops and some 4,700 were with the regular army blockading Gibraltar.

We must note the exceptional, excellent and persistent work of the officers and men of the Spanish corps of Royal Engineers and the Spanish corps of Royal Artillery throughout the Great Siege. The fortifications erected at the Spanish lines and at the Neutral Grounds were, on the whole, good examples of military engineering as it stood in the second half of the 18th century. The Spanish gunners, both on land and sea, certainly cannot be blamed for lack of effort. During the siege, it is estimated that they fired 244,104 rounds on Gibraltar from land batteries with a further 14,283 from gunboats for a total of some 258,387 shots, the majority being heavy-calibre cannon balls and mortar bombs. All this averaged some 195 shots per day so that, during periods of heavy bombardment, it 'rained bombs' on the town of Gibraltar, which was largely destroyed. In spite of such spirited efforts on the part of the Spanish gunners, the British casualties were relatively light and, although the damages to the sea-level fortifications could be substantial at times, they could be repaired quickly and were never breached. British batteries sited further up on the Rock's cliff were harder to hit and generally did not suffer substantial damages.

The dismal role of the allied naval forces, and the Spanish Navy in particular, during the operations in the area of Gibraltar between 1779 and 1783, is probably the greatest single factor to the siege's failure. French ships and squadrons wandered in and out of the area but this was really the domain of the Spanish Navy, which could count on its largest naval base at nearby Cadiz. The Spanish Navy was then the third strongest in the world and should have been capable of sealing the Rock. Yet, in spite of the Spaniards deploying numbers of ships-of-the-line, British squadrons slipped in and out of Gibraltar

RIGHT **Grenadier, Betschart Swiss Regiment, 1780.** The Spanish Army featured several Swiss regiments and Betschart's was part of the forces deployed against Gibraltar. Swiss regiments in Spanish service had blue uniforms that were distinguished by various regimental facings, yellow with white metal buttons in the case of Betschart. The Spanish infantry was armed with the .69 calibre Model 1757 musket, which featured brass mountings, and its bayonet. (Anne S.K. Brown Military Collection, Brown University, Providence, USA. Author's photo)

FAR RIGHT **Private of the Ultonia Irish Regiment in Spain (left) and gunners of the Spanish Army Artillery (centre) and the Marine Artillery (right), 1777.** Irish units recruited from Catholics in Ireland appeared in the Spanish Army in the early 18th century. Like the Irish in French service, they wore red coats. From 1775 to about 1782, Spanish infantrymen wore a leather cap with brass badges. The gunners of the Spanish forces gave possibly the most distinguished service of their country's forces during the Great Siege. They were relentless in their efforts against an almost impossible target whose defenders enjoyed exceptional cover. They wore a blue uniform with scarlet facings, the naval gunners having lapels, and had tricorn hats rather than helmets. (Anne S.K. Brown Military Collection, Brown University, Providence, USA. Author's photo)

relatively easily, as did dozens of individual ships flying the Union Jack. The only sizeable engagement was between Rodney's and Langara's squadrons in January 1780, which 'Moonlight Battle' ended in a resounding British victory. The most effective aspect of the Spanish naval effort was certainly Admiral Barcelo's light cruisers. As early as January 1780, Eliott could report that 'no vessel has got in here, the Spanish cruisers are so vigilant, consequently no supplies – our provisions daily consuming – many inhabitants near starving' (CO 91/26). However, small gunboats could certainly not block the great fortress all by themselves.

THE FRENCH FORCES

After the fall of Minorca in 1782, the four French infantry regiments that had taken part in that conquest joined the Spanish troops blockading Gibraltar from the month of June. This corps consisted of the white-coated Lyonnais and Bretagne regiments who were recruited in France, and of the 'dark sky blue'-coated Royal-Suèdois and Bouillon regiments who were mainly recruited with German soldiers. These infantrymen did not have much opportunity to distinguish themselves in the trenches outside Gibraltar. The really important contribution came from the numerous French staff officers that arrived on the outskirts of the Rock with the Duc de Crillon's appointment to overall command of the besieging forces. For the well-heeled and fashionable scions of the French military nobility, Gibraltar was the 'in' place to be as the only war operation going on in Europe. As it was a siege, it offered little danger, apart from the front line in the peninsula separating the Rock from Spain. Being situated in fashionable Andalusia, French officers flocked to this pleasant area in such numbers that some had to be sent back home.

BOTTOM, LEFT **French engineer officer in the uniform used from 1775 to 1786. This was blue with black velvet facings, scarlet piping, waiscoat and breeches, gold buttons, epaulettes and hat lace. The groups of French engineers led by the Chevalier D'Arçon were possibly the most severe threat to the Rock during the Great Siege. They sought innovative ways to overcome Gibraltar's tremendous defences. (Anne S.K. Brown Military Collection, Brown University, Providence, USA. Author's photo)**

BOTTOM, CENTRE **Grenadier private of the Bretagne Regiment, c. 1779–85. Bretagne was one of four regiments in the French force sent to help the Spaniards against the British in Minorca and Gibraltar. Bretagne, which originated in the province of Brittany, was one of the senior and most renowned regiments of the French Army. Its white uniform had crimson facings and yellow metal buttons. French infantrymen were armed, in principle, with the .69 calibre Model 1777 musket with its bayonet, although some units may still have had older models. (Watercolour by Hoffman. Anne S.K. Brown Military Collection, Brown University, Providence, USA. Author's photo)**

LEFT **Grenadier private of the Lyonnais Regiment, c. 1779–85. Lyonnais was part of the French force sent to Minorca and Gibraltar. Lyonnais, sometimes called Lyonnois, wore the white uniform typical of the French infantry. By the 1779 dress regulations, the regimental facings were pink lapels and cuffs, white metal buttons. The red epaulettes, hat tuft and moustaches were the distinctions of French grenadiers. They also carried hangers, as did NCOs and corporals in all French infantry companies. All NCOs carried muskets, halberds having been phased out in the early 1760s. (Watercolour by Hoffman. Anne S.K. Brown Military Collection, Brown University, Providence, USA. Author's photo)**

RIGHT **Grenadier private of the Royal-Suèdois Regiment, 1779.** In spite of being called 'Royal Swedish', this regiment was in the German establishment of the French Army by the 18th century. Like all German regiments in French pay, it wore 'dark sky blue' coats. Royal-Suèdois had yellow-buff facings with yellow metal buttons. Royal-Suèdois took part in the siege of Minorca before joining the forces blockading Gibraltar in 1782. (Plate after Isnard. Private collection. Author's photo)

FAR RIGHT **Grenadier private of the Bouillon Regiment, 1779.** This regiment was on the German establishment of the French Army and thus wore 'dark sky blue' coats. Bouillon had white facings with yellow metal buttons. The regiment took part in the siege of Minorca before joining the forces blockading Gibraltar in 1782. (Plate after Isnard. Private collection. Author's photo)

While the ageing Duc de Crillon did not offer very exciting leadership, he was not an outright opponent to new ideas. The younger staff officers certainly brought in much needed energy. Most notable were the engineers under the leadership of the Chevalier D'Arçon. Thanks to him and his assistants, the novel plan of the floating batteries was brought about as a way to break the deadlock, which the Spanish seemed unable to do. Had the original plans of the French engineers been respected and, most of all, the Spanish Navy been effective as a force, the Gibraltar garrison might have been defeated.

The French Navy, which was at one of its finest moments in its long history at the time of the American War of Independence, detached ships and squadrons to Gibraltar from time to time. These seem to have been more aggressive than their Spanish counterparts but they came under the overall command of the cautious Spanish senior command. Gibraltar and Minorca were considered a Spanish responsibility by the French Navy, which had taken a warlike stance against British fleets in America and the Indian Ocean.

OPPOSING PLANS

The initiative that resulted in the Great Siege had its origin at the court of King Carlos III in Madrid. It was (and remains) a basic matter of Spanish national policy not to abide by article X of the 1713 Treaty of Utrecht. As relations with Great Britain worsened during the late 1770s, the prospect of regaining Gibraltar and Minorca once again surfaced in diplomatic and military planning at court. The king and his prime minister, the Conde de Floridablanca, drafted up a wide-ranging strategic plan. Envoys and dispatches ran back and forth between Paris and Madrid to broadly outline the areas of military operations. For Spain, the emphasis would be, in America, to oust the British from the east bank of the Mississippi Valley and the territories bordering the Gulf of Mexico, and in Europe, to retake Gibraltar and Minorca. The French would attack the smaller British West Indian islands and the British in India as well as send an expeditionary force to the United States. In Europe, both countries would collaborate to threaten the English Channel and to chase the British out of the Mediterranean.

Apart from the failure of the combined French and Spanish fleets to make a powerful impression on the English Channel during 1779–80, the strategic plan worked fairly well for the Spanish in America. Thanks to the energetic Bernardo de Galvez, the British were defeated on the Mississippi and, by 1781, had surrendered all places on the American coast of the Gulf of Mexico (present-day states of Mississippi, Alabama and the western part of Florida). British raids in Central America had also been repulsed. The European front was the one that caused, if not concern, at least some worries.

As soon as war was declared by Spain on Great Britain, on 16 June 1779, dispatches were hurried south from Madrid and, five days later, Governor Eliott was notified that Gibraltar was under siege. The operations began in a leisurely way for some months. The strategic planning may have been agreed upon in Madrid but, initially at least, Gibraltar was not a priority that had been actively prepared for in advance. It took many weeks for a decent number of Spanish regiments to arrive on the scene, although far from sufficient to have any hopes of succeeding. It was not until 1782, when the Spanish camped outside Gibraltar were reinforced by other contingents as well as a French force, that a truly formidable army could offer a real threat.

From past experience, there were four ways to take Gibraltar: by intense bombardment, by treachery, by hunger and disease and by direct assault, such as the British had successfully mounted in 1704. All had been tried and failed thereafter. All these means presupposed that a tight naval blockade would be in place. In 1779, the so-called naval blockade was equally deficient in resources, the Spanish commander being provided with a squadron only slightly superior to the British naval force in Gibraltar. It was only thanks to small and fast cruisers, the Spanish commander's local initiative, that an impression was made on ships coming in and out of the Rock. Again, as with the land forces, the detailed planning to carry out the strategic objectives determined by King Carlos III was lacking.

When it became apparent that Gibraltar was not about to surrender through discouragement or starvation, the Spanish resorted to heavy bombardment but, although the town was largely destroyed, the fortifications remained formidable. No breaches were made and there was no inclination to plan an assault with ladders; the masses of charging Spanish infantry would have suffered losses that were considered too high to bear. The most innovative and threatening menace came with the French concept of the floating batteries. After their destruction, in September 1782, there were no further plans other than hope to use the large Spanish naval squadron to starve the garrison into surrender, but even that did not prevent Admiral Howe's convoy from slipping in.

For Britain, the retention of Gibraltar was also a matter of national policy. It may have cost up to £200,000 a year to maintain with little revenue in return, but it offered unrivalled commercial advantages for British trade in the Mediterranean as well as diplomatic and military influence. Minorca also had these advantages, but to a much lesser degree, and it did not have the strategic location or the symbolic importance of the Rock. In British military strategy, Minorca was expendable, whereas Gibraltar had to be retained at all cost. The only effective way to succeed in doing this was to keep the place supplied with sufficient food, troops and ammunition and therefore the British government made sure that the supplies got through. Three successive large convoys supplied Gibraltar over the years, raising the morale of the garrison while demoralizing the Spanish and French. The local details were left to Governor Eliott whose planning, as seen by the sortie and the defence against the floating batteries, was more than a match for that of his adversaries.

THE GREAT SIEGE

BLOCKADED

Spain's determination to re-take the Rock by force of arms had been trumpeted about for ages. A secret agreement regarding military assistance from the French to achieve this objective had even been signed in April 1779. Yet, curiously, when the chips were down and hostilities declared in June 1779, there was little military preparation in southern Spain. The blockade of Gibraltar announced on 21 June, with great flourish and courtesy by LtGen Joaquin de Mendoza to Governor Eliott, initially amounted to little more than an interruption of the mail by land.

That day, Capt Spillbury of the 12th Foot started his journal of the Great Siege by noting that

> the communications shut with Spain, the guards are reinforced, and Grand Battery made into a Captain's Guard. The pickets are ordered to be accoutred with their arms loaded … The heaps of sand on the Isthmus to be levelled by the Jews and Genoese of the Garrison, and no one to remain in the Garrison but those who have property, or will resist in defending it. Most of the men off duty employed repairing, &c., the works.

On 3 July, four men from each battalion company of the 12th, 39th, 56th and 58th regiments 'and six from the 72nd are attached to the Artillery'. Certainly, from the very first day, Governor Eliott was turning Gibraltar into a redoubtable armed camp and fortress.

On the Spanish side, for all the bombastic announcements about Gibraltar made in the last three-quarters of a century, it took over a month for a sufficient number of Spanish troops to arrive at the Rock. Gibraltar was really under a tight land blockade only from 18 July. The following months and years saw increasing numbers of Spanish troops camped outside Gibraltar.

When the Spanish announced the blockade, on 21 June 1779, the British garrison at Gibraltar was as follows:

Royal Artillery: 485
12th Foot: LtCol Trigge 599
39th Foot: Maj Kellet 586
56th Foot: Maj Fancourt 587
58th Foot: LtCol Cochrane 605
72nd Foot: LtCol Gledstanes 1,046
Hardenberg's Hanoverian: LtCol Hugo 452

A squad of the 25th Foot, 1770s. The uniform worn by British infantrymen on dress parade at Gibraltar and Minorca was generally as shown in this copy by Cecil C.P. Lawson of a picture of the 25th Foot in Minorca in the early 1770s. The main difference is that, by about 1780, the bayonet belt worn around the waist would likely be slung over the right shoulder and that short gaiters were worn. Going from the left, an officer armed with his spontoon, a grenadier and a file of soldiers of a 'Battalion' company. The regimental facings of the regiments in Gibraltar were yellow for the 12th and the 25th, green for the 39th, purple for the 56th, black for the 58th, white for the 59th, blue for the 72nd, buff for the 73rd and light blue for the 97th. (Anne S.K. Brown Military Collection, Brown University, Providence, USA. Author's photo)

Centre of the 1770s King's colours of the 12th Foot. Following the Great Siege, Gibraltar's motto with its coat of arms was granted as a distinction to this regiment as well as to the 39th, 56th and 58th regiments. The three Hanoverian regiments also added 'Mit Eliott zu Ruhm und Zeig' (With Eliott to Glory and Victory) on their colours. (From Milne's *Colour and Standards*. Author's photo)

Reden's Hanoverian: LtCol Dauchenhausen 444
de la Motte Hanoverian: LtCol Schleppegrell 456
Engineers and Company of Artificers: 122

This came to a total of 5,382 army troops. Naval forces accounted for another 760 officers and men but this could vary according to ships' movements and, at this point, were not reckoned as being part of the garrison. There were in addition about 1,500 military dependents, consisting mainly of soldiers' wives and children.

Gibraltar's civilian population was 3,201 persons according to a 1777 census. It was a cosmopolitan mix consisting of 519 British residents, 1,819 Roman Catholics native to the Rock, Portugal, Genoa and Spain as well as 863 Jews. There were also some Moroccans, perhaps between 300 and 400, who were not included in the census. Governor Eliott thought there were suspicious characters amongst them but his main concern was that they consumed food and other resources essential to a garrison under siege as well as being something of a hindrance to military operations. They were therefore strongly encouraged to leave and every vessel sailing from the Rock had civilian passengers.

By early October 1779, the Spanish had established a sizeable force opposite Gibraltar. British intelligence reckoned that 16 infantry battalions and 12 squadrons of cavalry amounting to about 14,000 troops were present. Such a number of men living in a relatively remote and barren area raised supply problems for the Spanish. There could not be enough food produced from the immediate countryside to fully supply such an army and inflation initially ran wild in the Spanish camps until adequate supply logistics were put into place. This probably explains why more troops were not sent immediately. The Spanish army was sufficient to tightly seal Gibraltar's land access and build lines of field fortifications

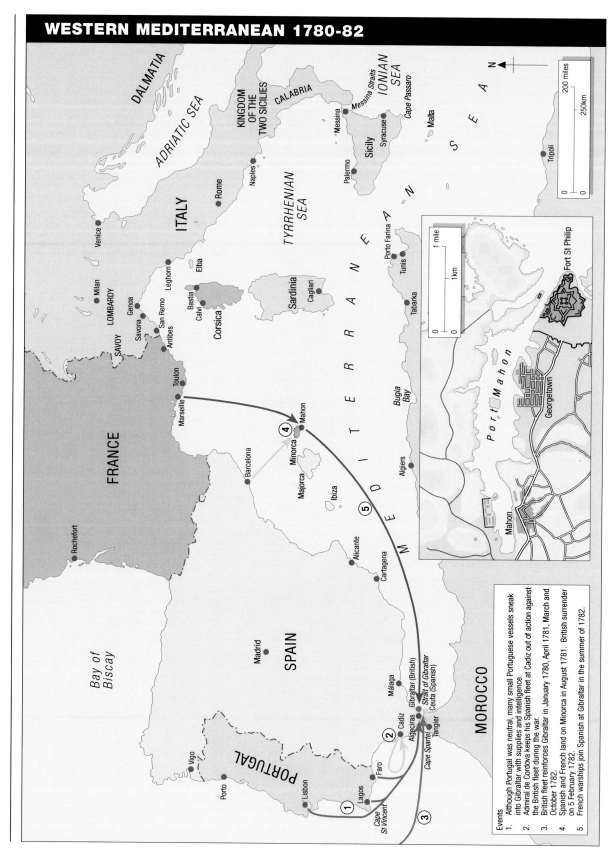

200 miles
250km

DALMATIA

ADRIATIC SEA

CALABRIA

KINGDOM
OF THE
TWO SICILIES

Messina Straits

IONIAN
SEA

Messina

Cape Passaro

Sicily

Malta

Palermo   Syracuse

Naples

Rome

ITALY

Tripoli

Venice

*TYRRHENIAN
SEA*

Milan

LOMBARDY

Genoa

SAVOY   Savona

San Remo

Antibes

Leghorn

Elba

Bastia

Calvi

Corsica

Sardinia

Cagliari

Porto Farina

Tunis

Tabarka

*Bugia
Bay*

1 mile

1km

Fort St Philip

Georgetown

Port Mahon

Mahon

Toulon

Marseille

FRANCE

Rochefort

Mahon

④

Minorca

⑤

Barcelona

Majorca

Ibiza

Algiers

M E D I T E R R A N E A N   S E A

Alicante

Cartagena

*Bay of
Biscay*

Madrid

SPAIN

Málaga

Gibraltar (British)

Strait of Gibraltar

Ceuta (Spanish)

Algeciras

②

Cadiz

Tangier

Cape Spartel

MOROCCO

Vigo

PORTUGAL

Porto

Lisbon

Faro

Lagos

①

*Cape
St Vincent*

③

34

GIBRALTAR 1779—83: BRITISH & SPANISH POSITIONS

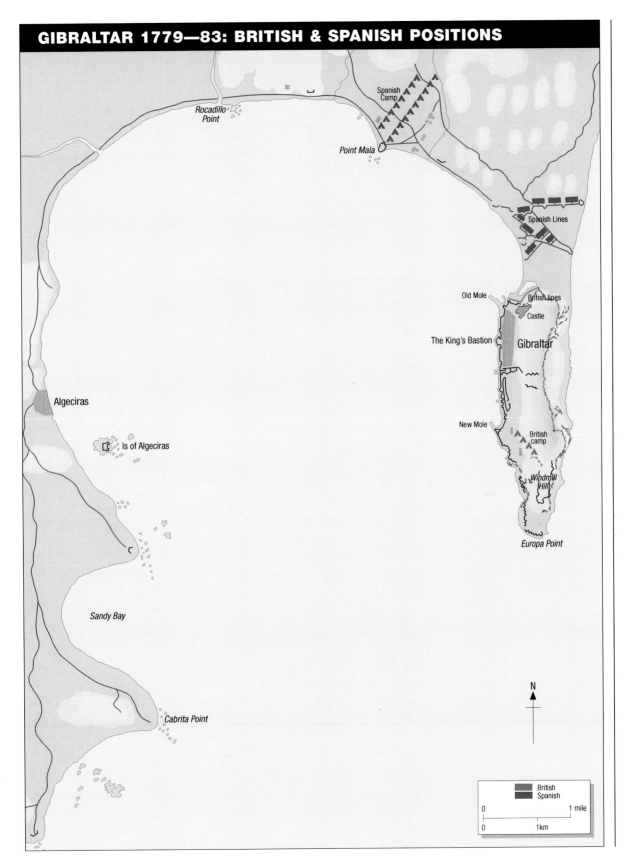

Spanish Camp

Rocadillo Point

Point Mala

Spanish Lines

Old Mole

British lines

Castle

The King's Bastion

Gibraltar

Algeciras

Is of Algeciras

New Mole

British camp

Windmill Hill

Europa Point

Sandy Bay

Cabrita Point

N

British
Spanish

0   1 mile

0   1km

Private of the 25th Foot wearing a white undress single-breasted jacket with red collar, cuffs and wings edged with yellow lace. Several units in Gibraltar and in the West Indies were issued white jackets. The men of the 72nd, for instance, had 'a white jacket turned up with blue.' This private is probably from the grenadier company as he has a cut-down bearskin cap. The 25th served Gibraltar from 1782 until 1793. Infantrymen were armed with the .75 calibre Short Land Pattern 'Brown Bess' musket with its bayonet. (Plate by Cecil C.P. Lawson after a period watercolour. Anne S.K. Brown Military Collection, Brown University, Providence, USA. Author's photo)

and trenches, but it was still much too weak to mount an assault. To have even a chance of taking a fortress, according to 18th-century practices, a besieging army was recommended to have at least three or four times the strength of the defending garrison, and this was no ordinary fortress.

To starve out Governor Eliott and his men made political sense. As much as Spain wanted Gibraltar back, there could be political tremors if the human cost were too high or, even worse, if an assault were to be defeated by the British. No one wanted a bloodbath.

The key, therefore, lay in the Spanish Navy's capacity to impose a sea blockade as effective as the army's land blockade. This was the only way Gibraltar could be truly sealed and brought to its knees. A rough and ready pursuer of Arab pirates, V Adm Antonio Barcelo, was called in but, from the start, he was never given the proper resources to effectively do the job. While a great Spanish fleet was sitting in nearby Cadiz during the autumn of 1779, all Barcelo had at his disposal was his 74-gun flagship, a small 50-gun ship-of-the-line and a fluctuating assortment of frigates, small gunboats and arab-style 'Xebecs'. In order to watch *all* sides of Gibraltar's peninsula, he would have needed at least three times as many ships so as to have two or three large ships at sea at any time with many more of the rapid small boats as well. As it was, his small squadron was in potential danger from the few Royal Navy ships in Gibraltar, including a ship-of-the-line, so he had to watch in as well as out.

Fast British, Gibraltarian, neutral and even North African ships quickly realized they could beat the Spanish naval blockade with a bit of daring and they continued to enter and leave Gibraltar, although not without risk. Barcelo was certainly at watch but, without enough guard ships that could be out at all times, it was a frustrating exercise as shown by an incident that occurred on 14 November 1779.

That day, the besieged were treated to quite a spectacle. A cutter was seen rapidly heading for Gibraltar on a westerly breeze. She was the *Buck*, a British privateer of 24 9pdr guns under the command of Capt Fagg. Seeing this, the Spanish made the signal of an enemy in sight and, rather amazingly, almost the whole of Admiral Barcelo's ships went after the British privateer. The Spanish ships consisted of a 50-gun ship and a 74-gun ship, the latter with V Adm Barcelo on board, a frigate of 40 guns, two xebecs, a gunboat of 14 guns and 21 smaller craft. Seeing this, the *Buck* headed south, was duly followed by the Spanish ships, and then turned to the windward while nearly all the Spanish vessels were carried east by the Straits' current. Only V Adm Barcelo's 74-gun flagship, which came last, managed to turn round to wait for the wily privateer as he was coming in, pursued by the 50-gun ship, which had also succeeded in tacking to the windward. The *Buck* now headed straight for Gibraltar's batteries and soon came within their range. In Gibraltar, everyone was on the ramparts watching the outcome of the pursuit. It was settled when the British batteries opened up on the approaching Spanish ships, which then fired a couple of broadsides towards the *Buck* as they turned around. The cutter was not hit and 'insultingly returned the Spanish Admiral's fire with her stern chase' before making her triumphant entry into Gibraltar's harbour.

On 20 November, the *Buck* sailed out, easily eluding the Spanish ships. But these were dangerous waters and, sometime later, the cutter's luck ran out when she came up against a French frigate. After a few broadsides, the *Buck* was taken but thereafter sank from the damage received.

Most ships sailing in and out did not make such a spectacular show but were just as effective at running past the Spanish blockade. Many of these 'blockade runners' were Portuguese under various disguises. They might fly British or other colours, have a Portuguese crew with an English captain or vice-versa and many other combinations. Portugal was officially neutral during the American War of Independence but it leaned towards its ancient British ally. Since the Middle Ages, these two maritime nations had often united their forces against their common Continental opponents. In Portugal's case, the ancient perennial enemy was Spain. Only a few years before the Great Siege, both countries had been at war with epic battles fought mostly in southern Brazil and present-day Uruguay between 1775 and 1777. Britain's rather cool and neutral stance in that struggle had naturally favoured Portugal's non-involvement from 1779. Nevertheless, not only was it in Portugal's interest that Gibraltar remain British, but additionally, there was no love lost in Portugal for the despised Spaniards and every Portuguese was hoping for their defeat at the Rock. All this was a recipe for considerable and shadowy intrigue from both sides and 'neutral' Lisbon became a hotbed for spies and secret diplomats of all sorts, much as it would again during the Second World War. Insofar as Governor Eliott at Gibraltar was concerned, some of his best intelligence and dispatches came via Lisbon on fast Portuguese boats, an often overlooked element that nevertheless cannot be dissociated from his successful defence of the Rock.

For the remainder of 1779, the garrison was basically blockaded while the Spanish were building fortifications and batteries outside. Ships were slipping in and out but V Adm Barcelo's fast cruisers nevertheless had an effect as large and slow-moving merchant ships full of provisions would not risk running past them. Governor Eliott's report to Lord Viscount Weymouth on 10 December gave a good summary of the situation in Gibraltar.

Regarding fortifications, LtCol Green had 'completed the Royal battery on the top of the North Rock for the three guns, and one of these on the same level to the last, which with two at Middle-Hill, and the batteries at Europa' now protected 'navigation and anchorage at the back of the Rock'.

An increasing worry was food. During the autumn, Governor Eliott warned authorities in Britain of the dangers of running out of provisions. By now flour, beef and peas would 'last for about five months for the garrison only'; there was no more oatmeal, butter and oil in store, wheat & rice would last for 'about six weeks'. The civilian inhabitants were about to run out of bread, 'except those who have any in their private stores'. Water was also scarce. As for the Spanish works outside, they had now mounted 'about 50 24pdrs [cannons], 43 mortars, one third for sea service 13in, all upon the platforms, ready for service – not a shot yet fired' (CO 91/25).

On 8 January 1780, Governor Eliott wrote again to Lord Viscount Weymouth mentioning that 'no vessel has got in here, the Spanish cruisers are so vigilant, consequently no supplies – our provisions daily consuming – many inhabitants near starving … we have wine or strong liquor for near four months only' (CO 91/26). The underlying message

Officer and private, 1st Battalion, 5th or de la Motte's Hanoverian Regiment, *c.* 1785. The battalion at Gibraltar was commanded by Maj von Schlepegrell. Col La Motte was at Gibraltar, serving as a brigadier. De la Motte's had yellow facings. (Private collection. Photo by A.U. Koch)

Officer and private, 1st Battalion, 6th or Hardenberg's Hanoverian Regiment, *c.* 1785. This regiment, which had previously fought side by side with the 12th Foot at the battle of Minden in 1759, was again with the 12th during the sortie from Gibraltar in November 1781. The battalion at Gibraltar was commanded by LtCol von Bussche. Hardenberg's name changed to von Sydow in 1782. It had very dark green facings. (Private collection. Photo by A.U. Koch)

Adm George Rodney. His fleet not only provided relief and supplies to Gibraltar in January 1780 but also defeated a Spanish fleet off Cape St Vincent. (Author's photo)

BOTTOM, LEFT **V Adm Juan de Langara commanded the Spanish fleet that was defeated by Adm Rodney at the 'Moonlight Battle' off Cape St Vincent on 7 and 8 January 1780. Wounded and captured on his flagship, the brave Adm de Langara was brought to Gibraltar to recover. After the war, he was instrumental in fostering Spanish scientific explorations and naval surveys in the northern Pacific. (Museo Naval, Madrid)**

BOTTOM, RIGHT **Prince William Henry, second son of King George III and future King William IV, was a midshipman on board Adm Rodney's fleet. The captured Spanish Admiral Langara was amazed to see him going about his duties and commented that: 'Well does Great Britain merit the empire of the sea, when the humblest stations in her Navy are supported by Princes of the Blood', according to Capt Drinkwater. The prince came ashore at Gibraltar on 20 January 1780, which provided considerable encouragement to the garrison. (James Kochan Study Collection, Frederick, Maryland)**

was clear. If Gibraltar could not be supplied from England, it would have to surrender – possibly without having fired a shot – within a few months.

ADMIRAL RODNEY'S RELIEF, JANUARY 1780

In Britain, the message had been heard. On 29 December 1779, a large convoy escorted by a strong Royal Navy squadron of 21 ships-of-the-line under the command of Adm Sir George Rodney sailed from England for Gibraltar. On 15 January 1780, a fast brig flying British colours went right past the Spanish vessels and batteries and came into Gibraltar with news that this large relief fleet was on its way. Everyone at the Rock was elated but then wondered if they would get past the Spanish fleet. The Spanish, too, had learned that a convoy was sailing for Gibraltar and, initially believing a weak squadron escorted it, detached Adm de Langara with 11 ships-of-the-line to intercept it from the Mediterranean while Adm de Cordova's 15 ships in the Atlantic would also try to catch the British ships. More recent intelligence soon reached de Cordova as to the actual size of the British squadron. He now realized he was heavily outnumbered and went into Cadiz. Meanwhile, de Langara's squadron crossed the straits into the Atlantic, expecting to meet a British squadron of equal strength with de Cordova's fleet on its heels.

On 14 January, de Langara's ships sailing west now saw Rodney's large squadron sailing east towards him. He made a run for Cadiz, hoping to slip by the pursuing British ships but the Royal Navy ships had copper-covered hulls, which made them fast. By four in the afternoon, they caught up with the Spanish squadron that fought bravely into a moonlit night until two in the morning. Adm de Langara,

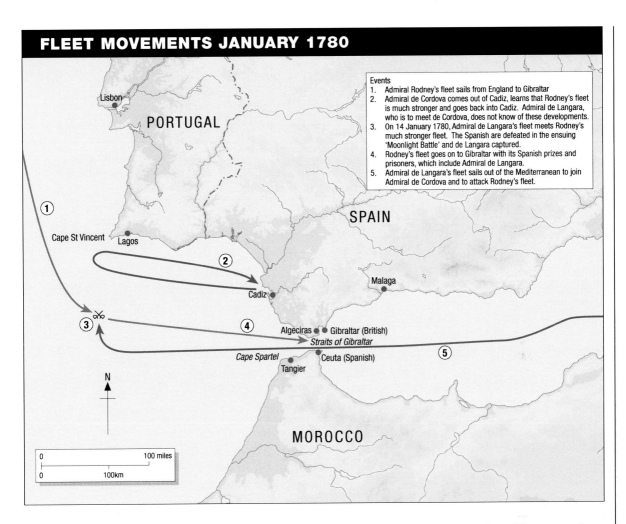

PORTUGAL

Lisbon

Cape St Vincent
Lagos

SPAIN

①

②

Cadiz

Malaga

③

④

Algeciras ● Gibraltar (British)
Straits of Gibraltar

⑤

Cape Spartel Ceuta (Spanish)
Tangier

N

MOROCCO

0   100 miles
0   100km

Events
1. Admiral Rodney's fleet sails from England to Gibraltar
2. Admiral de Cordova comes out of Cadiz, learns that Rodney's fleet is much stronger and goes back into Cadiz. Admiral de Langara, who is to meet de Cordova, does not know of these developments.
3. On 14 January 1780, Admiral de Langara's fleet meets Rodney's much stronger fleet. The Spanish are defeated in the ensuing 'Moonlight Battle' and de Langara captured.
4. Rodney's fleet goes on to Gibraltar with its Spanish prizes and prisoners, which include Admiral de Langara.
5. Admiral de Langara's fleet sails out of the Mediterranean to join Admiral de Cordova and to attack Rodney's fleet.

on board his flagship, the 80-gun *Fenix*, and five other ships were taken; a seventh blew up. British prize crews were put on board and all sailed for Gibraltar.

From 19 January, the relief fleet arrived at Gibraltar with its prizes amidst artillery salutes and cheers. The Spanish wounded, which included Adm de Langara, were landed. Governor Eliott greeted Admiral de Langara and Prince William Henry who was serving as a midshipman on the British fleet. That the king's son was actually in Gibraltar was a great boost to the garrison's morale, which was already quite good. The old governor remarked that the prince was 'in perfect health, and has often gone over great part of the works, and makes very just observations, both on our defences and the Spanish designs'. Adm de Langara, for his part, was impressed to see a prince doing the humble duties of a midshipman. He and his officers, no doubt rather dejected, spoke 'with great rancour against the French, and say, that neither the king [of Spain] or the minister, were inclin'd to the war' (CO 91/26).

The bay of Gibraltar was almost full of British ships by 25 January when Adm Rodney arrived. They unloaded all sorts of supplies. The 2nd battalion of the 73rd Highland Regiment was also on board, intended for Minorca, but Governor Eliott wanted them to stay at the Rock. Adm

Rodney had the authority to alter orders if circumstances permitted and he agreed. The 73rd, numbering 36 officers, 72 NCOs and 944 rank and file under the command of Col George McKenzie, joined Gibraltar's garrison instead.

In spite of all the supplies brought, there was no wine or rum and this would be 'severely felt' by the soldiers whose health, according to Governor Eliott, could be affected if their drinking habits were upset. Considering he himself only drank water, Governor Eliott was remarkably sensitive to the lifestyle of his soldiers and deplored the want of strong liquor.

FIRESHIP ATTACK

The blockade continued after the fleet's departure. Shortly after midnight, on 7 June 1780, the watch on HMS *Enterprise*, which was anchored off the New Mole, spotted movement to the west that proved to be several sails in the distant dark. The mysterious vessels were challenged but, instead of answering, erupted into fireworks and flames: these were six Spanish fireships sailing in a crescent formation and intent on setting fire to the British ships. Three of the burning Spanish vessels were linked by chains. Capt Lesley of HMS *Enterprise* immediately ordered his ship's cables cut and fired three guns rousing the garrison. Soon, the batteries on the New Mole, HMS *Panther* and other vessels were firing at the Spanish fireships, which slowed them down, while navy officers and seamen in longboats 'with their usual intrepidity' rowed to the fireships, grappled them and towed them out of harm's way. It was a close call regarding the largest of the Spanish fireships; it probably would have entered the harbour and got among the British transport vessels 'had not a few bars-shots, from a thirty-two pounder at the Mole-head, turned her round and the current carried her into Rosia Bay.'

The garrison was certainly excited and the state of alarm kept up until dawn when it was clear there would not be a second wave of fireships. Although foiled, the attack did 'justice to the ingenuity of Don Barcelo', as it was well planned and his squadron had been, Drinkwater relates, 'judiciously stationed at the entrance of the Bay, to intercept our men of war in case they had attempted to escape from the fire-ships'.

During 1780, many small ships and fast boats came in from nearby Morocco, bringing fruits and vegetables. To make the blockade really effective and starve out the garrison, Spanish diplomats were hard at work at the court of the Emperor of Morocco and managed to outbid the British with promises and gifts by the end of the year. Moroccan ports were closed to British vessels as they were effectively rented to the Spanish. On 11 January 1781, two of the emperor's vessels arrived in Gibraltar under a flag of truce. They landed the British consul with 109 British residents and sailors that had been detained in Morocco. This was bad news, if not unexpected, for Governor Eliott and the garrison. Already, scurvy had broken out because of the lack of fruit and a shortage of the most essential food was looming in spite of reduced rations. There was beef until March, peas, butter and olive oil until April, bread until June and pork until July. There were also supplies of cheese, rice, wheat and dried raisins but these alone could barely suffice for a basic diet and, by August, would also be expended. Vessels sneaking in from Portugal or other places would never fill the gap and, in a dispatch of 18 January to the government all written in cipher, Governor Eliott urgently asked for supplies with 'all possible expedition' on a large fleet for 'a general and very extensive relief' (CO 91/27).

VICE-ADMIRAL DARBY'S RELIEF FLEET, APRIL 1781

The shortage of foodstuffs for the garrison and the inhabitants was quite serious by the end of March 1781. Some small ships had come in, but what was needed was a very large supply and it was now over a year since any sizeable shipment had reached Gibraltar. At that time, soldiers were on a reduced weekly ration consisting of 5 ½ pounds of bread, 13 ounces of salt beef, 18 ounces of salt pork, 2 ½ ounces of butter, 12 ounces of raisins, half a pint of pease, one pint of Spanish beans. The garrison could 'subsist starvingly' but the civilian inhabitants felt distressed. The Spanish blockade seemed to be working.

On 12 April, numerous sails flying the Union Jack entered Gibraltar Bay; it was V Adm George Darby's Royal Navy squadron of 29 ships-of-the-line escorting nearly 100 store-ships from England laden with supplies for the Rock. The Spanish fleet had been totally unable to intercept Darby's relief.

The Spanish troops besieging Gibraltar were very frustrated and, for the first time during the Great Siege, opened fire with all their mortars and batteries. The ships went further south and unloaded their supplies at the South Mole, out of range of the Spanish batteries. V Adm Darby's relief fleet unloaded all supplies, leaving even all the black powder from the warships that could be spared since Governor Eliott expected to have many artillery duels from then on. The Spanish kept up such a fire that the town of Gibraltar rapidly suffered extensive damage from the bombs and the ensuing fires. Some discipline broke down amongst the troops when soldiers ransacked ruined houses and shops, discovering hidden supplies of food and drink. This would occur time and again during the Great Siege in spite of the harshest punishments and public executions sanctioned by the governor. All civilians and dependents on the Rock that could embark on the fleet, probably about a thousand souls, did so and V Adm Darby sailed for England on 21 April.

THE SPANISH BATTERIES

By April 1781, the Spanish had built an impressive number of batteries facing Gibraltar across the peninsula. Besides the older forts of San Felipe (27 guns) and Santa Barbara (23 guns) at each end, there now were the:

King's, or Black, Battery: 14 guns
Infanta Battery: 7 guns

The image at the top of the page shows two pages of a manuscript journal with handwritten notes and a sketch of the Spanish lines.

Prince's Battery: 14 guns
Princess's Battery: 14 guns

And about 50 mortars mounted in the lines and at the San Carlos Battery for a total of some 114 pieces of artillery. All were heavy-calibre 24pdr cannons and 12in mortars.

From then on until late 1782, their firings were often daily and massive. The Spanish artillery barrages soon destroyed much of the town, which, in terms of 18th-century warfare, was regarded as inhumane by the British. However, the British were not immune from this sort of behaviour either, as shown by their destruction of much of Quebec City by bombardments in 1759. The Gibraltar fortifications, however, were never seriously affected by the Spanish bombardments. Governor Eliott made it a standing order to return their fire whenever expedient, notably when workmen were seen in the Spanish forward lines and batteries on the isthmus.

A view of the Neutral Grounds from the Land Port in November 1781. Gibraltar Bay is at left. A narrow causeway leads to the Bayside Barrier. To its right, the Inundation and, further right, a road leads to Forbes's Barrier. Further away, the newly constructed Spanish forward lines. Still further back, the Spanish main lines with, at their left end, Fort San Felipe and, at their right end, Fort Santa Barbara. (Print after Drinkwater. Author's photo)

THE SORTIE

Grenadier of the 58th Foot, 1770s. This regiment arrived in Gibraltar in 1770, served as part of its garrison during the Great Siege and returned to Britain in 1784. The regimental facings were black and its men's white lace had a red stripe. The officers had gold buttons and lace. Grenadiers were distinguished by bearskin caps, wings at the tip of the shoulders, brass match cases and hangers. The regimental clothing of the 58th was reported as 'good' in March 1777 except that the shoulder knots to denote the rank of corporal were 'a mixture of red and white instead of all white' (WO 27/39). (Plate by R.D. Coldwell after a c.1769 rendering. Author's photo)

On 15 September 1781, the Spanish 'began a line, in three zig-zags' approaching the Rock and worked 'only by night' to avoid British artillery fire. By 9 October, this 'new line of approach' seemed to establish a parallel, which was accordingly done. By 15 November, three batteries had been completed near the western shore and, Governor Eliott reported, 'the enemy continues his line of approach to the eastward', adding that British fire had 'killed and wounded a great number of their men' (CO 91/27).

The Spanish lines slowly but surely crept in closer during the following days. As soon as a new parallel trench was dug, workmen would start building a battery, guns would be brought in and, before too long, the Spanish artillerymen would be firing on the town. The Spanish field works were solidly built and, while not invulnerable, withstood quite well the return fire from the British. By the third week of November, the Spanish had completed their advanced batteries and fired a storm of cannon balls, bombs and shells on the British, which caused substantial damage to the town and put some strain on the garrison. A battery with two mortars and six cannons was named San Pascual and another mounted with cannons called San Martin. The most annoying fire came from heavy ordnance in a 12in mortar battery named San Carlos.

Governor Eliott was aware that this could seriously affect the morale of his men and, therefore, acting on information about the advanced positions brought in by two Spanish deserters, he decided on a very bold move – to make a sortie.

In siege warfare, the besieged might choose to detach a large body of the garrison to make a raid on the enemy's siege works. The move was defined as a 'sortie' by the French, which meant getting out, and the word was incorporated into several other languages, including English.

Governor Eliott's idea was to strike out, take and destroy the positions and get back into Gibraltar as safely as possible. To have the maximum chance of success, secrecy was all-important. Therefore, the governor told no one about his plans. The enterprise was certainly a risky one for, if it was considered near suicidal for the Spanish to attack Gibraltar across the isthmus, the same could be said for the British attacking the other way. Should the Spanish learn of the intended sortie and set a trap that destroyed the raiding party, it could weaken the garrison and its resolve to the point that it might consider surrender as its only option.

At this time, the Spanish army outside Gibraltar was estimated to have as many as 12,000 men. There were rumours that more troops were on the way and that, with naval support, an all-out assault would be attempted on the Rock. This, together with the constant bombardment of the advanced batteries, might be discouraging to the Rock's defenders. On the other hand, Governor Eliott calculated, a successful raid would be a great boost for his garrison's morale, which needed to show it could strike out as well as endure the enemy's bombardments.

What really mattered to Governor Eliott was how many men might be in the Spanish forward lines and how many might be close enough in the main lines, 600 metres to the north, to actually be able to march out. From what could be gathered from various sources, the Spanish lines and the nearby camp might have about 12,000 men. It was clear that all of the latter could never muster quickly enough to march out to repulse a sortie's attack on the forward lines. As nearly all the Spanish Army seemed to be much further back and only a relatively small force of 'fifty or sixty cavalry and six hundred infantry' was in the forward and main lines, a strong British raiding party ought to be able to overcome the Spanish troops defending such works as the San Carlos Battery, destroy the enemy's advanced positions and rush back into Gibraltar before Spanish reinforcements arrived (CO 91/27). Thus, the risk was substantial but the Spanish forward lines might be taken quickly as they had been built with two faults that were noted by the British. As they were intended for artillery, banquettes had not been made for their garrison to step up the trench to fire at an attacking enemy and they had no redans to cover their flanks. A determined surprise attack in the night, therefore, had good chances of success.

Discretion was certainly essential for such an operation and Eliott made his preparations in great secrecy. On the Spanish side, with no hint of any British movements, things were relatively relaxed, even in the forward lines, especially as the third week of November featured bad weather. This greatly favoured Governor Elliott's plans.

On the evening of 26 November, the evening gun was fired as usual in Gibraltar and the gates officially closed for the day, a routine that was kept up during the whole siege. Normally, guards were changed and some troops would go on duty and others come off it. This time things were different. All troops were ordered to their quarters and the taverns and all liquor outlets in town were closed. New orders now came and these specified a certain number of units and detachments to assemble with the greatest discretion at midnight on the Red Sands. Fire fagots and working tools were brought. The officers selected to conduct the sortie having been briefed and instructed, the raiding force assembled under the command of BrigGen Ross and was divided into three columns. The troops selected by Eliott were:

Left Column under LtCol Trigge
12th Foot: 26 officers and 458 other ranks
58th Foot, Light Infantry: 3 officers and 60 other ranks
72nd Foot, Grenadiers: 4 officers and 106 other ranks
72nd Foot, Light Infantry: 4 officers and 106 other ranks
Royal Artillery: 1 officer and 39 other ranks
Sailors: 2 officers and 103 other ranks
Engineers: 1 officer
Total: 41 officers and 872 other ranks

Centre Column under LtCol Dachenhausen
39th Foot, Grenadiers: 3 officers and 60 other ranks
39th Foot, Light Infantry: 3 officers and 60 other ranks
56th Foot, Grenadiers: 3 officers and 60 other ranks
58th Foot, Grenadiers: 3 officers and 60 other ranks
73rd Foot, Grenadiers: 4 officers and 106 other ranks
73rd Foot, Light Infantry: 4 officers and 106 other ranks
Royal Artillery: 2 officers and 44 other ranks
Engineers and workmen: 6 officers and 164 other ranks
Total: 28 officers and 660 other ranks

Right Column under LtCol Hugo
56th Foot, Light Infantry: 3 officers and 60 other ranks
Reden's, Grenadiers: 3 officers and 78 other ranks
La Motte's, Grenadiers: 3 officers and 78 other ranks
Hardenberg's: 16 officers and 330 other ranks
Royal Artillery: 1 officer and 27 other ranks
Engineers and workmen: 4 officers and 330 other ranks
Total: 30 officers and 903 other ranks

Grand total: 99 officers and 2,435 other ranks

The battalion companies of the 39th and 58th regiments, who would provide the reserve support, were assembled on the Grand Parade at the same time to 'sustain the sortie if necessary'.

Each soldier was to have 36 rounds, each musket with a good flint in the hammer and a spare flint in the pocket of the soldier, no swords were to be carried and only two drummers per regiment were included in the force.

The plan was that the Right Column would go ahead and strike first at the parallel ending the Spanish advanced works. It would be followed shortly by the Centre Column, which would hit the enemy's forward entrenchments at its San Carlos mortar battery further west. Lastly, the Left Column would hit the gun batteries at the advanced fortifications on the western shore. BrigGen Ross led the attack. By two in the morning of 27 November, the moon was setting and it was a dark night; 45 minutes later all troops of the raiding party now advanced without making noise. The deepest silence was observed by officers and men as the three columns approached the enemy lines. All in the columns were in great spirits and eager to strike a blow on the Spaniards.

In the Spanish advanced lines, the sentries stationed before the works were on the lookout. Sure enough, those near the old gardens on the Neutral Grounds spotted the movements of the Right Column. They fired their muskets in the air to give the alarm and ran back to their lines. The alarm now spread as Spanish drummers in the forward lines beat to arms. The Right Column did not give them much time as LtCol Hugo ordered it to move fast towards their objective. They closed in rapidly with fixed bayonets and the few Spanish troops in the works retreated, knowing they could not resist the onslaught. The end of the parallel, which was the east flank of the Spanish advanced works, was thus easily taken.

A company of Hardenberg's Regiment (from the Right Column) got lost in the dark, mistook its target and found itself in front of the San Carlos Spanish mortar battery, whose sentries fired at the Hanoverians.

THE SORTIE, 27 NOVEMBER 1781 (pages 46–47)

The 99 officers and 2,435 NCOs and privates that rushed out of Gibraltar would generally have been as shown in this plate. It was a clear night and getting darker as the moon was setting as the three columns of troops were hurrying to their assigned targets. The officer and grenadiers shown could be of almost any regiment, with dark facings on the red uniforms. The officer wears a laced hat and has the two epaulettes on his shoulders that distinguished regimental senior officers (1). His commissioned status was also indicated by the gold (or silver, depending which regiment) buttons and laced buttonholes of his scarlet coat (2) and by the crimson silk sash worn round his waist that reveals him

to be British (3). Hanoverian officers had the same type of uniform except for a gold silk sash. Grenadiers were distinguished by the 1768-model grenadier bearskin cap (4), shoulder wings on their coats (5) and brass match cases on their cartridge box shoulder belts (6) to denote their elite status. British infantrymen were armed with the .75 calibre Short Land Pattern musket with its bayonet (7). All figures are shown with the short black gaiters (8) that were worn by Gibraltar's garrison. They are running towards the Spanish forward works whose outer sentries have started to fire at the rapidly approaching shadows in the night. In a few minutes, the British will charge in and take the works. The Rock, although distant, forms an overbearing background (9) to this remarkable sortie. (Patrice Courcelle)

The only solution was to storm it and, in a gallant rush, Hardenberg's men climbed the 18ft high parapet, went into the works, shot and bayoneted anyone there and easily took the San Carlos Battery. The survivors of its meagre Spanish garrison ran off.

The Centre Column then arrived at the San Carlos Battery, one of its targets. At the head of the column were the flank companies of the 39th Foot who initially thought Hardenberg's men inside the battery to be Spaniards since they had no idea it was already taken. Colonel Dachenhausen, who was with flank companies of the 39th, ordered them to fire and several men of Hardenberg's were hit. Shouts in German and/or English, added perhaps to the glimpse of red coats in fire flashes, quickly raised doubts as to the identity of the men inside. The 39th stopped shooting and, thanks to passwords, Hardenberg's men were identified. It was a minor 'friendly fire' incident and the arrival of the Centre Column was a relief to Hardenberg's company as the position was much more secure and safer in the event of a Spanish counter-attack.

LtCol Trigge's Left Column edging the seashore met some slight resistance as it approached its objective. The flank companies of the 72nd charged ahead and quickly took the batteries of San Pascual and San Martin next to the western shore, putting their few Spanish defenders to flight. Both the flanks and the centre of the Spanish advanced works were now taken and the rest of the trenches were abandoned.

The British were now in complete possession of the Spanish forward lines, with their artillery batteries, ammunition magazines and stores of supplies. It was an outstanding success. At the San Carlos Battery, to everyone's surprise, Governor Eliott had come out, joined the raiding party there, and was looking at the scene with much satisfaction. When Gen Ross came up, Eliott asked him: 'What do you think of the business, is it not extraordinary that we have gained the Enemy's work so easily?' To which Ross replied: 'The most extraordinary thing is to see you here!'

The forward sector of the Spanish front lines had been caught unprepared for such a sizeable raid. Some officers and men fought bravely but, on the whole, the Spanish did not put up much resistance to the overwhelming British force. In the ditch of the San Carlos Battery, a badly wounded Spanish artillery captain lay dying and refused to be moved. Governor Eliott himself came to try to persuade him, but to no avail; he asked to be left alone to 'perish amid the ruin of my post'. His dying words were reported to be: 'At least one Spaniard shall die honourably.'

A few Spaniards were taken prisoner and the keys to the ammunition magazines were found on a captured Spanish artillery officer, Lt Vincente Freire, who had been wounded. The other officer captured was Lt Baron von Helmstadt of the Walloon Guards, who was badly wounded in the knee. Initially, he refused medical help from the British but eventually relented. Sixteen soldiers were also captured and all were taken into Gibraltar, the wounded being sent to hospital. According to Drinkwater, the Spanish only had a captain, three subalterns and 74 men in the forward lines when the British made their sortie. They belonged to the blue-coated Walloon Guards and the artillery.

As planned in the event that the Spanish works would be successfully attacked and taken, part of the British troops consisting of the 12th Foot and Hardenberg's took up positions between the captured works and the

THE SORTIE ON THE SPANISH FORWARD LINES, 27 NOVEMBER 1781

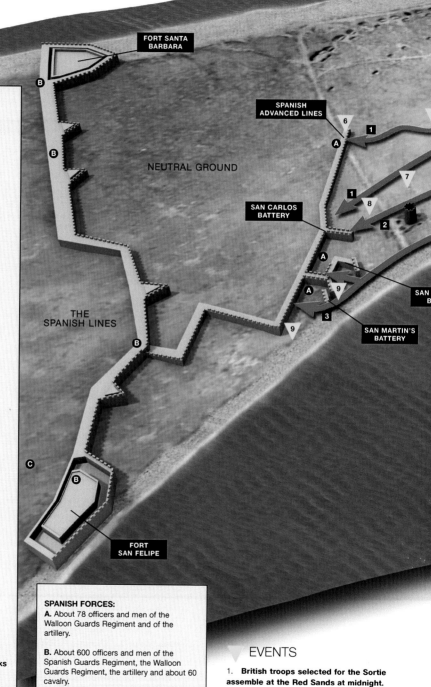

FORT SANTA BARBARA

SPANISH ADVANCED LINES

NEUTRAL GROUND

SAN CARLOS BATTERY

THE SPANISH LINES

SAN MARTIN'S BATTERY

SAN F BA

FORT SAN FELIPE

BRITISH FORCES:

1. Right Column (LtCol Hugo)
56th Foot, Light Infantry:
3 officers and 60 other ranks
Reden's, Grenadiers:
3 officers and 78 other ranks
La Motte's, Grenadiers:
3 officers and 78 other ranks
Hardenberg's:
16 officers and 330 other ranks
Royal Artillery:
1 officer and 27 other ranks
Engineers and workmen:
4 officers and 330 other ranks
Total: 30 officers and 903 other ranks

2. Centre Column (LtCol Dachenhausen)
39th Foot, Grenadiers:
3 officers and 60 other ranks
39th Foot, Light Infantry:
3 officers and 60 other ranks
56th Foot, Grenadiers:
3 officers and 60 other ranks
58th Foot, Grenadiers:
3 officers and 60 other ranks
73rd Foot, Grenadiers:
4 officers and 106 other ranks
73rd Foot, Light Infantry:
4 officers and 106 other ranks
Royal Artillery:
2 officers and 44 other ranks
Engineers and workmen:
6 officers and 164 other ranks
Total: 28 officers and 660 other ranks

3. Left Column (LtCol Trigge)
12th Foot:
26 officers and 458 other ranks
58th Foot, Light Infantry:
3 officers and 60 other ranks
72nd Foot, Grenadiers:
4 officers and 106 other ranks
72nd Foot, Light Infantry:
4 officers and 106 other ranks
Royal Artillery:
1 officer and 39 other ranks
Sailors:
2 officers and 103 other ranks
Engineers:
1 officer
Total: 41 officers and 872 other ranks

Grand total: 99 officers and 2,436 other ranks

4. In reserve: the battalion companies of the 39th and 58th regiments.

SPANISH FORCES:
A. About 78 officers and men of the Walloon Guards Regiment and of the artillery.

B. About 600 officers and men of the Spanish Guards Regiment, the Walloon Guards Regiment, the artillery and about 60 cavalry.

C. Some 11 to 12,000 officers and men.

▼ EVENTS

1. **British troops selected for the Sortie assemble at the Red Sands at midnight. Fire faggots and work tools are brought. The raiding force is under the command of BrigGen Ross. The troops are divided into**

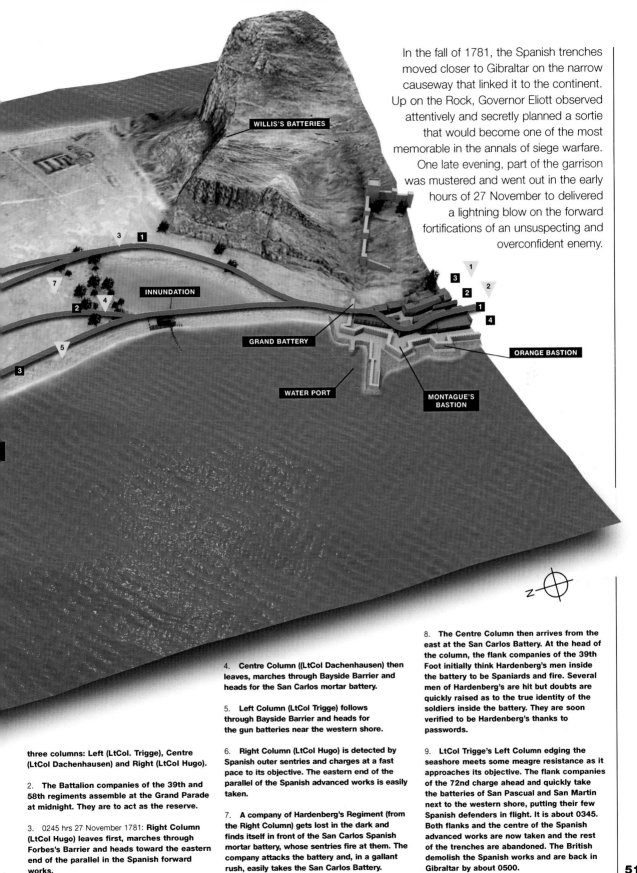

WILLIS'S BATTERIES

In the fall of 1781, the Spanish trenches moved closer to Gibraltar on the narrow causeway that linked it to the continent. Up on the Rock, Governor Eliott observed attentively and secretly planned a sortie that would become one of the most memorable in the annals of siege warfare. One late evening, part of the garrison was mustered and went out in the early hours of 27 November to delivered a lightning blow on the forward fortifications of an unsuspecting and overconfident enemy.

INNUNDATION

GRAND BATTERY

ORANGE BASTION

WATER PORT

MONTAGUE'S BASTION

three columns: Left (LtCol. Trigge), Centre (LtCol Dachenhausen) and Right (LtCol Hugo).

2. The Battalion companies of the 39th and 58th regiments assemble at the Grand Parade at midnight. They are to act as the reserve.

3. 0245 hrs 27 November 1781: Right Column (LtCol Hugo) leaves first, marches through Forbes's Barrier and heads toward the eastern end of the parallel in the Spanish forward works.

4. Centre Column ((LtCol Dachenhausen) then leaves, marches through Bayside Barrier and heads for the San Carlos mortar battery.

5. Left Column (LtCol Trigge) follows through Bayside Barrier and heads for the gun batteries near the western shore.

6. Right Column (LtCol Hugo) is detected by Spanish outer sentries and charges at a fast pace to its objective. The eastern end of the parallel of the Spanish advanced works is easily taken.

7. A company of Hardenberg's Regiment (from the Right Column) gets lost in the dark and finds itself in front of the San Carlos Spanish mortar battery, whose sentries fire at them. The company attacks the battery and, in a gallant rush, easily takes the San Carlos Battery.

8. The Centre Column then arrives from the east at the San Carlos Battery. At the head of the column, the flank companies of the 39th Foot initially think Hardenberg's men inside the battery to be Spaniards and fire. Several men of Hardenberg's are hit but doubts are quickly raised as to the true identity of the soldiers inside the battery. They are soon verified to be Hardenberg's thanks to passwords.

9. LtCol Trigge's Left Column edging the seashore meets some meagre resistance as it approaches its objective. The flank companies of the 72nd charge ahead and quickly take the batteries of San Pascual and San Martin next to the western shore, putting their few Spanish defenders in flight. Both flanks and the centre of the Spanish advanced works are now taken and the rest of the trenches are abandoned. The British demolish the Spanish works and are back in Gibraltar by about 0500.

main Spanish lines. This was to provide a defence should the enemy be able to quickly mount a counter-attack. Meanwhile, the engineers, artificers, workmen and sailors had followed the troops into the captured positions. Their work was to destroy as much of the fortifications as quickly as possible. They had come carrying tools and fire faggots, the latter to set alight the magazines and stores. In the captured batteries, mortars and cannons were spiked and made utterly useless. The works were turned to rubble in record time as the British artificers and workmen furiously hacked away at them. The area was now being illuminated as columns of fire engulfed the magazines and, as the British retreated, became a fiery cloud as the flames, which made an impressive sight, consumed the front lines. Its savage beauty was not lost to Governor Eliott who called out to his men: 'Look round, my boys, and view how beautiful the Rock appears by the light of glorious fire.' It made such a reflection in the night that, as Drinkwater later wrote, the troops and objects in the general area were 'beautifully illuminated' forming a view 'not possible to be described'.

In the Spanish camp, all were shocked and dismayed at the enormous fire that was now burning their advanced lines, which had been so difficult to put up, into a pile of burned rubble. The great fire lighted up the area and, with the Rock as a backdrop, redcoats could be seen hurrying back into Gibraltar. The Spanish gunners in the main lines opened up but, in their excitement, aimed for the town and the upper batteries rather than the area beyond the Neutral Grounds where the raiders were, all without much effect. The nearly invulnerable British upper batteries high up the Rock, on the other hand, delivered a withering fire on the main Spanish lines and forts below.

Governor Eliott and his officers during the sortie of 27 November 1781. At left, the British troops and workmen destroy the captured Spanish works. At the centre lying on the ground, the mortally wounded Walloon Guard captain. At right, from left to right: Ensign A. Mackenzie (in Highland dress), Governor Eliott, Lt G.F. Koehler, LtCol J. Hardy, BrigGen C. Ross, Capt A. Witham, Capt R. Curtis, LtCol T. Trigge and LtCol Hugo. (Print after John Trumbull. Anne S.K. Brown Military Collection, Brown University, Providence, USA. Author's photo)

The Spanish reaction was anything but what Governor Eliott could reasonably expect. The best bet was that, in about an hour's time or so, thousands of Spanish troops would have been mustered and would start to advance to retake the forward lines and, if possible, trap the raiders in the process. Nothing like that happened. The only activity coming from the Spanish lines consisted of about 40 Spanish cavalrymen, which appeared to the east of Hardenberg's Regiment posted between the main Spanish lines and the captured forward lines now being destroyed. Governor Eliott was nearby and ordered two companies of Hardenberg's to take position and face them. The Spanish cavalry did nothing further. Indeed, it seems that General Alvarez had planned nothing substantial for countering a sortie and, certainly, even if there were plans, nothing was done.

It was now 3:45 in the morning and, although it was increasingly clear to General Ross and Governor Eliott that the Spanish were not about to mount a counter-attack, it was high time for the British to get back into Gibraltar. By then, the British gunners and engineers were ready to blow up the advanced lines. Soon, the dawn's early light would start to light up the area and the raiders would make much better targets for the Spanish gunners. As planned by Eliott, the 12th Foot and Hardenberg's stayed in their positions to cover the retreat of the other infantrymen, gunners, workmen and sailors. All went back into town without any incidents. The 12th Foot then retreated through the Bayside Barrier, between the Inundation and the sea, without a hitch. Hardenberg's was to retreat through Forbes's Barrier, further east. Finding its gate locked and no one to open it, the regiment went around the Inundation and through the Bayside Barrier. As the last men were safely coming into Gibraltar, tremendous explosions creating mushrooms of smoke and debris destroyed what was left of the Spanish forward lines. It was five in the morning, 'just before the break of day' wrote Governor Eliott. One of the most famous sorties in British military history had come to an end.

British casualties in the sortie were very low. Only four men had been killed, 25 wounded (including an officer) and one missing. Hardenberg's had nearly half of the casualties with two killed and 12 wounded. Nothing had been lost, not even a musket or a tool, except that a man of the 73rd later claimed to have lost his kilt! Such light losses were utterly surprising to Eliott and his officers. They expected higher casualties for a raiding party that had gone over a kilometre out of its base and within a few hundred metres of the main Spanish lines that were armed with over 100 guns.

Spanish casualties were probably not much higher, although Governor Eliott reported that 'many were killed upon the spot' before giving way 'with great precipitation'. Besides the utter destruction of their 'stupendous' works, 'two mortar batteries of ten thirteen inch mortars, and three batteries of six guns each … were spiked, their beds and platforms destroyed' (CO 91/27).

All of the Spanish forward line burned during the morning of 28 November with, Spillbury observed, 'some loaded shells going off' from time to time. After their initial surprise, the Spanish regained their composure somewhat and, no doubt rather upset, on the signal of a rocket opened up a withering fire from 'cannon, small arm, &c.' on the town but to little avail.

THE SIEGE OF MINORCA

Early in 1781, the courts of Spain and France came to an understanding regarding a joint expedition to take Minorca. The Conde de Floridablanca agreed with the Duc de Vergennes that Spain would provide most of the forces that would be joined by a French division. The overall command was given to the Duc de Crillon, certainly the best choice, as he had served with both armies.

Naval superiority was achieved in early July 1781 when the powerful French Atlantic squadron of 22 ships-of-the-line under Adm Guichen joined a Spanish fleet of 36 ships-of-the-line under Adm Luis de Cordova in the western Mediterranean. The British were certainly unlikely to challenge such a powerful fleet in that area.

The Spanish contingent embarked on the fleet at Alicante and Cartagena in mid-July. The force consisted of the Burgos, America, Murcia, Princesa, Saboya, Ultonia (Irish) and 1st Catalonian infantry regiments, and also the Lusitania, Sagunto and Villaviciosa dragoon regiments with artillery and engineer detachments, which landed on Minorca on 20 August. The train of artillery consisted of 54 cannons and 18 mortars. In early October the Swiss infantry regiments of Bettchard and Ehrler, the dragoon regiments of Almanza and Numencia with detachments from the Rey, Mallorca, Millan infantry and Sagunto dragoons, reinforced the Spanish troops in Minorca. Within 15 hours, the Spanish army had marched across the island and occupied its three ports. The combined fleet then departed but a Spanish squadron under Adm Moreno was left in the area to blockade the island. In the middle of October, a French corps of over 3,800 men consisting of the Lyonnais, Bretagne, Royal-Suèdois and Bouillon infantry regiments, with detachments of artillery, engineers and additional artillery landed on Minorca. Mshl de Crillon's army now amounted to 14,297 men.

Against such an army, there was little that Governor James Murray could do with the forces he had at hand. The British garrison of Minorca consisted of three companies of the Royal Artillery, the 51st and 61st regiments, Prinz Ernest's and Goldacker's Hanoverian battalions, seamen and marines landed from the ships at the island and a few volunteers. In all about 2,700 regular officers and men. The whole island certainly could not be defended and Murray withdrew into Fort St Philip, situated on a peninsula at the entrance of the port city of Mahon. This citadel was no Gibraltar but was nevertheless an extremely strong fortification. Its centre was the 16th-century Fort St Philip to which had been added a maze of ditches, bastions and other outworks as well as some outlying forts.

The place, if well defended by its garrison, would require a long siege and this was exactly what Governor Murray and his men resigned themselves to. There could be only two outcomes: the first was to hold out until a British fleet came to relieve the place, a rather faint possibility; the

James Murray was governor of Minorca, the other British base in the western Mediterranean. He was an experienced soldier, had been one of Wolfe's brigadiers at Quebec and the first British governor of Canada before assuming the governorship of Minorca in 1774. Hopelessly outnumbered and cut off by a large Franco-Spanish force from August 1781, he nevertheless put up a stubborn defence for six months before capitulating in February 1782. (From a c. 1790 print. Author's photo)

second was to hold out as long as possible in the hope that this would help their comrades in Gibraltar. If the French and Spanish forces could be kept fighting on two fronts, it would be that much less pressure on Gibraltar in spite of the vast forces simultaneously arrayed against the two British citadels of the Mediterranean.

By 20 August, the citadel of Fort St Philip had been invested and its garrison henceforth totally surrounded. Before the start of the siege operations, Mshl de Crillon invited Governor Murray to surrender, as was the custom of the age between opposing commanders. Murray of course rejected the summons. So the siege was on. Mshl de Crillon seems to have believed that the British garrison had up to 7,000 men, which indicates either faulty intelligence or some diplomatic scheming by the marshal who added that 'Spanish valour' would compensate for the insufficient numbers of the besieging force. Governor Murray soon put them to the test in early September when, in a daring sortie, he destroyed a Spanish battery and captured over a hundred men. In any event, the arrival of the French contingent in September brought the necessary superiority in numbers, which was more than enough to cope with the actual strength of the British garrison.

From 15 September, Fort St Philip was submitted to relentless bombardments, day in and day out, but British casualties were relatively light in spite of a rain of bombs and shells. And the Franco-Spanish force did not attempt an assault to take parts of the fortifications. The strength of these works, which had 234 guns at the beginning of the siege, would have required a heavy toll in casualties for very minimal gains. In many ways, Governor Murray's enemies were more inside the fort than outside of it. Within the circle of senior officers, opinions were divided on how to carry out the defence, with one party siding with the governor and the other with LtGen Draper, the second-in-command. But the garrison's worse enemy was sickness. Vegetables and fruits soon ran out, with no possibility of replacement. In November, scurvy broke out amongst the garrison. Living in underground casemates that were damp and unhealthy also took its toll on the soldiers, who increasingly dragged themselves to mount guards. All the same, they were not about to give up and would occasionally be cheered by the arrival, and safe departure, of a British vessel. Amazingly, in spite of Admiral Moreno's ships, a few small vessels slipped in and out of Fort St Philip during the siege, providing news if little else. Thus, as in Gibraltar, the Spanish Navy was incapable of sustaining a tight blockade at Minorca.

Weeks and months passed with Spanish and French bombardments of the fort from the 15 batteries that surrounded it. The British gunners returned their enemy's fire as far as possible. For instance, Captain Dixon of the Royal Artillery noted on 9 January 1782 that 'they never stopped firing, and we as well returned it' and that it was observed that they would fire some '750 shot and shell every hour'. The gunners were understandably 'greatly fatigued'. By 28 January, the castle at the centre of the citadel was much damaged 'as well as the rest of the works, are in a most shocking sight.' Through it all, the whole garrison showed outstanding valour and especially the gunners who showed near-heroism daily. Three artillery NCOs were commissioned by Governor Murray, who constantly visited all the work, during the siege for their outstanding conduct. Indeed, Captain Dixon wrote that 'never was artillery better served, I may say in

Lt La Tour d'Auvergne-Corret became a near-legendary officer in Louis XVI's army due to his fighting qualities, daring and luck. Wanting to be where the action was, he went to Minorca in late 1781 and there was noted for his outstanding feats, which included the rescue of a wounded officer under fire during the siege of Fort St Philip. However, in January 1782, he was ordered back to France as he had left his unit, the Angoumois Infantry Regiment, without leave! (Print after JOB. Author's photo)

Fort St Philip at Port Mahon, Minorca, seen in the background during the early 1770s. The garrison's staff, with officers and other personnel of the 25th Foot are in the foreground. The elaborate defences of the fort that gave the Spanish and French considerable difficulties in 1781–82 can be seen. Anonymous contemporary ink and wash drawing. (Anne S.K. Brown Military Collection, Brown University, Providence, USA. Author's photo)

favour of our own corps.' Spanish gunners also knew their profession well and managed to knock out 78 British guns in Fort St Philip.

Through it all, the garrison's casualties were not too high but, with the opening of a new and sizeable Grand Battery on 4 February, Governor Murray knew that the end was near. By then, he only had about 660 soldiers still fit for duty and another 415 able to stand guard. Scurvy had reached epidemic proportions amongst the garrison, with 560 men afflicted with it in hospital. This was besides about 150 wounded and at least another 100 sick from other causes. The fort's damp and dark casemates were now crowded with over 800 weak and sickly men who could hardly stand up. A white flag was hoisted, firing ceased, the drummers beat a parley, emissaries from both sides met and the capitulation was agreed to. The Honours of War were granted by the Duc de Crillon. This notably provided for the garrison to march out 'with shouldered arms, drums beating, matches lighted and colours flying' for the ships that would take them to England.

At the appointed hour the following day, 600 men of the British garrison that could walk marched out of Fort St Philip between the ranks of Spanish and French soldiers. The British soldiers were in such a plight that it is said that many a veteran soldier in the allied camp shed a tear at the sight of these sickly but proud-looking men dressed in rags. The compassion and care displayed by Spanish and French troops to the unfortunate British soldiers and their dependents were qualities equally found in the British garrison of Gibraltar towards their stricken enemies. It was a most worthy trait of war of the 'Age of Enlightenment'. These laudable military qualities that attempted to humanize the terrible consequences of war have unfortunately been largely lost in our own time.

The British garrison had 59 killed (including two officers, both of the Marines) and 149 wounded (including 15 officers). Spanish losses came to 238 dead and 380 wounded, testimony to the sturdy walls of Fort St Philip and the good shooting of the British artillery. In all, 2,889 persons came out of the fort, including 154 women, 211 children and 43 English 'peasants' with the garrison.

The loss of Minorca was a setback for the British as their only base within the Mediterranean had fallen. It was especially bad news for Governor Eliott and everyone at Gibraltar. The forces of Spain and France would surely now combine to deliver the final blow to the British by taking Gibraltar.

GIBRALTAR HOLDS ON

In the meantime, life in Gibraltar went on with its usual restraints in the supply of food and the ongoing bombardments. During February 1782, in spite of the bad news from Minorca, the situation at the Rock improved somewhat thanks to vessels, mostly from Portugal, that arrived with their holds full of lemons and vegetables as well as eight British Ordnance vessels filled with ammunition and other warlike supplies. A boat from Faro, in Portugal, also brought in mail and intelligence about high casualties in the Spanish lines due to British artillery fire. It must have been true as British shells routinely set on fire the works in the Spanish advanced lines. Governor Eliott had the prisoners and the garrison's invalids leave on these ships and cheerfully reported on 20 February that 'the garrison grows daily more and more healthy' thanks to the citrus rations. The Spanish blockade seemed fairly lax but there were tense moments. For instance, the *Mercury*, a fast ship carrying wine and lemons out of Lisbon, narrowly escaped the Spanish cruisers that were firing at it until it came 'under our guns' (CO 91/28).

In March 1782, more ships arrived. Admiral Barcelo's squadron was reinforced with more frigates but British ships, too, were not without protection. HMS *Success*, a frigate escorting another vessel, engaged and burned a Spanish frigate off Gibraltar. On 22 March, two British frigates escorting four transports eluded the Spanish and came in. They disembarked the 97th Foot, 800 strong, as well as 'all the drafts and recruits for the several regiments, clothing for [the] Hanoverian Brigade, provisions, stores, &c., &c.', reported a happy Governor Eliott. The artillery duels continued over the Neutral Grounds in April with the British obviously having the upper hand; the Spanish works had been 'consumed' by the 'great precision' of the garrison's guns and the Spanish 'scarcely venture to show their heads from behind their works', commented Governor Eliott with obvious satisfaction at his gunners' work. In spite of that, supplies in food and ammunition were running low by May. Gunpowder and 10in shells were wanted as well as many food items and more 'portable soup' that had been lately sent to the hospital and proved to be 'of the greatest benefit'. The 97th Foot, which had arrived sickly, was improving in health so rations were obviously adequate and another Portuguese ship slipped in with oranges.

GIBRALTAR'S NAVY

Another initiative taken by Governor Eliott and his garrison was to actually increase the size of the naval force at Gibraltar. The Spanish gunboats having been really annoying, it was decided to give them some naval opposition to keep them at bay. As unlikely as it may seem for the

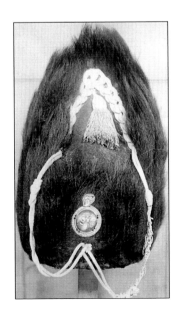

A back view of a grenadier's bearskin cap of the 97th Foot, *c.* 1780–83. This regiment arrived in Gibraltar in March 1782. Considering its short time at the Rock, this unit had a remarkably high proportion of casualties: 167 out of 1,231 for the garrison during the entire length of the Great Siege. The facings to its red coats were light blue. (Sumner note books. Anne S.K. Brown Military Collection, Brown University, Providence, USA. Author's photo)

besieged to do this, work on building new British gunboats started in April 1782. The material to do this was available, so why not? By 4 June, the king's birthday, the last of a dozen new British gunboats was launched amidst fanfare and artillery salutes. The new gunboats were:

Revenge, one 24pdr
Defiance, one 24pdr
Resolution, one 18pdr
Spitfire, one 18pdr
Dreadnought, one 18pdr
Thunder, one 18pdr
Europa, one 24pdr
Terrible, one 18pdr
Fury, one 18pdr
Scourge, one 18pdr
Terror, one 18pdr
Vengeance, one 18pdr

Each had a crew of 21 men detached from the frigates HMS *Brilliant,* HMS *Porcupine* and the cutter HMS *Speedwell.*

The new gunboats patrolled the shores of Gibraltar but, at night, 'curiosity often prompted them to approach the Enemy's shore' across the bay near Algeciras. These adventurous crews thus detected the progress of the construction of the floating batteries and, on 14 June, the arrival of a large French fleet of 12 ships-of-the-line under the command of Adm Guichen, bringing some 4,000 French troops to join in the siege.

THE DUC DE CRILLON AND THE FRENCH ARRIVE

By early 1782, there were at least 28,000 Spanish Army troops in the Gibraltar area, almost a third of the entire Spanish metropolitan army. The deadlock over the capture of Gibraltar, after two-and-a-half years of siege, was total: there was, in fact, no progress at all for the Spanish. At the headquarters of the French Army in Paris, the problems caused by Gibraltar's incredible resistance drew increasing attention. Apart from their tenuous naval blockade, the Spanish had done all that could be expected in 18th-century siege warfare to no avail, such was the strength of the Rock. It simply could not be approached and breached by the narrow strip of land separating it from the mainland.

Engineer Colonel D'Arçon had been pondering the problem for sometime out of personal interest. In March 1780, he had sent a proposal to the Spanish ambassador in France, the Count de Aranda, which outlined the use of indestructible floating batteries that would batter the weakest part of Gibraltar's defences, its western flank, making a breach that would allow assault troops in. Ambassador de Aranda noted the novel idea and brought it out in due course, as the French and Spanish were increasingly wondering what to do about the Rock. In July 1781, D'Arçon was sent to Gibraltar to see for himself and come up with a detailed plan.

His conclusion was that the area of the New Mole was the weakest point. He proposed that a landing be made there that would be

The battery south of the King's Bastion, built in 1773. This battery was one of the most active artillery areas as it was the main stronghold in the Line Wall. The sea, which came up to the wall's edge in the 18th century, was filled and built over in the 20th century. The Royal Artillery commanders at Gibraltar during the Great Siege were Col Goodwin until 1780, Col Tovey to November 1781 and Major Lewis. (Author's photo)

supported by a combined fleet and even designed special landing crafts with hinged bows that would come down to let troops out rapidly. A massive bombardment from the Spanish land batteries would keep the British occupied in the area of the Old Mole. The greatest innovation that would keep the British totally occupied and under intense bombardment at the King's Bastion and along the Line Wall was the deployment of ten massive floating batteries that would be so heavily armoured as to be unsinkable and which were also incombustible, even under the heaviest fire with red-hot shot. The plan called for massive resources. However, all could see that if resources were provided and the plan followed, it had a good chance of success.

The plan was first approved in Madrid and then by the French and Spanish courts. It effectively put Colonel D'Arçon and the French engineers in charge of the technical aspects of the operation. Plates were even printed in France of the bombardment maps and plans for the floating batteries. France would also send ships and troops to join the Spanish at Gibraltar. The Great Siege was coming into a whole new phase.

On 1 April 1782, a fast vessel came into Gibraltar from Portugal with urgent intelligence about the progress of the construction of the floating batteries. Furthermore, the Duc de Crillon was said to be on his way to take over command of the forces besieging the Rock. Governor Eliott and his senior officers could only guess at what would come next, but there was no doubt now that even harder challenges were ahead for the garrison.

On 9 May, the hulks of eight floating batteries were brought into Algeciras. Two days later, another Portuguese vessel brought intelligence confirming that the Spanish would be joined by the French troops that

A battery on the cliff at Willis's in action during the Great Siege. The British guns were, on the whole, well covered by various natural and man-made obstacles. Furthermore, many batteries were high up on the Rock's cliff. All this made effective counter fire by the Spanish gunners quite difficult. Thus, the British gunners enjoyed some relative safety as shown on this print. An artillery officer looks on in the company of an officer of the 73rd Highlanders. The officers of the 73rd wore a scarlet jacket with buff facings, silver buttons and lace, diced bonnets with black plumes, government tartan with buff and red over stripes. (Author's photo)

had been at Minorca and that Marshal de Crillon had assumed command. Gibraltar was to face an attack of unprecedented scale.

Meanwhile, the Spanish naval blockade was reinforced but remained difficult to apply fully. Three British storeships were taken by two Spanish frigates and three xebecs, but three more British ships slipped in and a Portuguese vessel holding 30,000 oranges made it to Gibraltar in May. This last shipment was valuable to combat scurvy, which had greatly receded.

Nevertheless, things were starting to look gloomy for the garrison. On 15 June, bad luck hit as a Spanish shell set fire to the magazine of Princess Ann's Battery at Willis's; it blew up killing 14 men and wounding another 15, but none of the latter 'dangerously'. In spite of the explosion, damage to the battery was 'very inconsiderable'. Perhaps even more disturbing was the sight of French frigates escorting about 70 transports carrying the French troops coming into Algeciras where another two large ships were being converted into floating batteries. Governor Eliott asked London for more troops and supplies to face a formidable attack 'that will probably commence soon.'

An inside view of Princess Amelia's Battery's 'Ship's timber caissons and splinter proofs' c. 1780. As can be seen, everything is in good order with artillery tools neatly stowed by hooks on the wall as a soldier sweeps the floor. (James L. Kochan Study Collection, Frederick, Maryland)

THE FRENCH TAKE OVER THE SIEGE OPERATIONS

The arrival of the French naval and military forces at Gibraltar was certainly encouraging to the Spaniards. The French navy was at one of the peak periods of its history and, with Admiral de Cordova's powerful Spanish squadron, should finally manage to seal the Rock completely. The French regiments joining the Spanish were veterans of the siege of Minorca so they were not 'green' troops that had never seen combat. All these reinforcements came at a price for the Spanish: the operations were henceforth under the command of Marshal de Crillon, of Minorca fame, with his staff and engineers that now had the last word in how the siege operations would be carried out.

Handing over command to the French was a conscious decision on the part of Carlos III and Conde Floridablanca. It was made to secure the collaboration of Louis XVI and Count Vergennes to expedite the re-taking of Gibraltar, a place that was 'in Spain'. After years of futile efforts by the Spanish forces, there was nothing else to be done. Mshl Crillon, with his long experience in the Spanish Army and as conqueror of Minorca was certainly the most logical choice that could be made from a political and military point of view. Both the Spanish and the French hoped that the new arrangements would lead to new and imaginative concepts to bring about success. In this they were not to be disappointed.

Unfortunately for Col D'Arçon, Mshl de Crillon also had a plan – or so he claimed, as a detailed plan from him has yet to be found – that was much more conservative. It would have involved sea and land bombardment with a landing by ships full of troops that would be scuttled on the Rock. The result was that Mshl de Crillon was rather lukewarm about the whole scheme with floating batteries and special landing boats. It also seems that the naval commander of the combined fleet, the cautious Adm de Cordova, was equally sceptical about Col D'Arçon's inventions. However, both senior commanders were tasked to carry out Col D'Arçon's plan, which had been approved by the highest authorities in Madrid and Versailles. Mshl de Crillon was none too happy about this and made his reservations known. This underlying discontent would have worked in favour of the British garrison. On the surface, however, everything was progressing with unbounded optimism and, to many in Spain and France, the fall of Gibraltar seemed a certainty.

The participation of the French in the siege aroused considerable public interest in France. Scores came down to the Gibraltar area, from princes to ordinary army officers taking leave, to see what would happen. It was, after all, the only prolonged military land operation taking place in Europe and it was taking place in an exceptional setting. As it was a static siege, there was no danger of great movement. A gentleman and his lady would be in no danger only a few kilometres away, leisurely watching the proceedings from the nearby hills while sitting in a shaded veranda, sipping a glass of wine with a snack of the delicious local olives. By the end of August 1782, there were increasing numbers of fashionable gentry making something of a 'Grand Tour' of southern Spain, taking up residence in the hills to see the bombardments and actions in and about Gibraltar a few kilometres to the south, a thrilling and yet perfectly safe activity.

The military population at the camp outside Gibraltar was also growing. In early September, the Spanish and French forces were now very numerous. The units present were:

For the Spanish:
Spanish Guards: 121 officers, 2,912 NCOs and privates
Walloon Guards: 115 officers, 2,912 NCOs and privates
Saboya: 31 officers, 689 NCOs and privates
Cordova: 31 officers, 688 NCOs and privates
Burgos: 63 officers, 1,377 NCOs and privates
Murcia: 63 officers, 1,377 NCOs and privates
Ultonia (Irish): 32 officers, 1,377 NCOs and privates
Voluntarios de Aragon: 23 officers, 387 NCOs and privates
1st Voluntarios de Cataluna: 45 officers, 1,805 NCOs and privates
Princesa: 31 officers, 688 NCOs and privates
Napoles: 63 officers, 1,377 NCOs and privates
Betschart (Swiss): 43 officers, 1,191 NCOs and privates
Grenadier companies: 66 officers, 1,338 NCOs and privates
Dismounted cavalry: 69 officers, 1,377 NCOs and privates
Dismounted dragoons: 66 officers, ? NCOs and privates
Provincial Militia grenadiers: 201 officers, 4,509 NCOs and privates
Royal Artillery: ? officers, 1,341 NCOs and privates
Dragoons and cavalry: 141 officers, 2,440 NCOs and privates

For the French:
Lyonnais: 61 officers, 1,024 NCOs and privates
Bouillon: 48 officers, 1,025 NCOs and privates
Bretagne: 61 officers, 1,016 NCOs and privates
Royal-Suèdois (German): 61 officers, 1,000 NCOs and privates

Total: 28,227 (including 1,314 officers).

This list is taken from d'Arçon's *Histoire du siège de Gibraltar* (Cadiz, 1783) to which should be added about 70 Spanish artillery officers and some 1,350 dismounted Spanish dragoons. Nor does it include Spanish and French staff officers, engineers, sappers, naval troops and sailors on shore. These added would total, at the very least, some 35,000 Spanish and French officers and men.

Within Gibraltar, Governor Eliott prepared his garrison as best as he could with the resources available to him. Although there was much activity in the Spanish batteries to the north, he considered that the strange craft being built in Algeciras would be used for an attack on the Rock's western walls and batteries. On 7 September, he deemed that an attack was imminent and ordered new postings to the garrison in an effort to strengthen defences along the western side. The Marine Brigade (900 men) was posted in the Europa and Little Point areas. The Flank Companies of the 39th were at the North Bastion; three companies of the 39th at the South Bastion; five companies of the 39th at Ragged Staff; the 72nd at the right of North Bastion town; the 73rd towards the South Bastion; Martin's artillery company at the Grand Battery and Waterport; Lloyd's artillery company at the King's and South bastions; Hanoverian

Brigade from the eight-gun battery south to Prince Edward's Battery inclusive; 56th at the South Parade; 12th at the New-Mole Parade; 97th at the Rosia Parade and the 58th in front of its encampment with a Flank Company at Windmill Hill. The engineers and artificers were in two divisions, one at Esplanade town and the other at Esplanade south. In this way, of the 7,500 men in the Gibraltar garrison in September (including about 400 in hospital), some 3,430 were always on duty as follows:

Guards: 1,091 officers and men
Picquets: 613
Working parties: 1,726 (exclusive of engineers and overseers)

This was apart from men on duty as assistants and orderlies in the hospital 'and in other departments of the garrison'. The available manpower was deployed to maximum capacity by Governor Eliott and his staff.

DESTRUCTION OF THE SPANISH FORWARD BATTERIES

Following the sortie, it took some time for the Spanish to reorganize their efforts towards advancing their lines nearer to the Rock. The Spanish engineers were not discouraged and, by March 1782, forward lines were creeping up again nearer to the British positions. At the end of the month, they made an especially concerted effort, extending their parallel within a hundred yards, 'with casks and fascines, banked up with sand in front', Drinkwater observed. By 29 March, they had dug more traverses with advanced batteries. The British gunners poured fire on the forward lines at double the rate of the Spanish fire but the brave Spaniards would not quit in spite of high casualties and, indeed, by early April, had the Mahon Battery up, which the British initially called the Eastern Battery. The Spaniard's new forward lines appeared complete but Governor Eliott bided his time. Perhaps he felt they were still too distant. He also had other worries on other fronts of the Rock, notably the increasing certainty of a naval attack, so that the forward lines on this front seemed relatively stable.

It must be observed that Governor Eliott was an exceptionally unexcitable tactician who would calmly handle the various probes made by the Spanish, choosing his time to retaliate. Although besieged and outnumbered, he kept as much initiative as possible, and, especially after the sortie, kept his enemies guessing as to what he would do next. As it turned out, he did nothing out of the ordinary about the Mahon Battery and the new forward line during the whole summer. The artillery firings on both sides had almost ceased since the end of June in the northern sector.

In early September 1782, the emboldened Spanish had again been relentless in advancing their lines. They were actually moving forward to the area where the British wanted them: so close that it would almost be a killing ground. Governor Eliott approved a suggestion by General Boyd to bombard these forward lines using red-hot shot and carcasses. There had been increasing use of such projectiles in the preceding months and the British gunners had become quite proficient with them. They were almost

Officer and private, 1st Battalion, 3rd or Reden's Hanoverian Regiment, c. 1785. The battalion at Gibraltar was commanded by LtCol von Walthausen. Hanoverian troops wore uniforms that were generally similar to those of the British Army, most notably the red coat. However, the officers had yellow silk sashes and their gorgets bore the horse badge of Hanover. Reden's had black facings. (Private collection. Photo by A.U. Koch)

Sketch of a fascine from a manuscript journal of the siege by Capt Drinkwater. (Private collection. Photo by Stephen Wood, Southsea)

Two large Spanish 13in mortars, the likes of which were mounted in the Spanish batteries to bombard Gibraltar. The sizeable bombs from such mortars contributed notably to the destruction of the town. These mortars, now at Fort Ticonderoga, USA, were both cast in Barcelona in 1724. (Author's photo)

intolerably hot in the near-tropical weather of a Gibraltar summer but the good results were most encouraging to the garrison. The red-hot shots had worked rather well on the Spanish gunboats in previous days and the British gunners were now called upon to test their growing expertise in this manner of firing guns. At seven in the morning of 8 September, everything was in place in all the British northern batteries. They now opened fire on the western part of the Spanish parallel and the shooting was 'supported through the day with admirable vivacity' by the British gunners. After a few hours of intense bombardment, the results became apparent and, to quote Drinkwater, 'exceeded our most sanguine expectations.' The Spanish Mahon Battery with adjoining works and parallel below were set on fire and consumed by night fall. The other batteries of San Carlos and San Martin were heavily damaged by breaches and had to be partly dismantled by the Spaniards and French.

It was an outstanding success, thanks to the expert use of red-hot shot fired from favourable positions. The Spanish and the French troops appeared disorganized on this occasion, although they were seen by the British on the Rock to have 'displayed astonishing bravery'. The French were thought to have lost 140 killed and wounded and the Spanish at least as many. General Boyd confirmed that the use of red-hot shot could indeed be formidable. Grates and furnaces were, by then, installed near all the batteries for that purpose.

General Boyd, although invalided by age and sickness, had watched and directed the British operation sitting in a chair through it all. Afterwards, as he slowly walked back to his quarters, he was saluted by all who saw him and cheered for his outstanding success. Relations between Governor Eliott and General Boyd, while rather cool, were always correct and gracious.

Spanish gunboat, 18th century. Small and fast gunboats carried out the most effective Spanish naval operations against Gibraltar, before and during the Great Siege. They came in many shapes and types, the one illustrated being the more conventional Spanish Navy type of the 1780s. (From a contemporary print. Author's photo)

THE GRAND ATTACK

With all the preparations going on in the allied camp during the last months, everyone knew that an extraordinary attempt would be made to take Gibraltar. Indeed, it was common knowledge all over southern Spain that the attack was imminent and, within a few days, some 80,000 people – an amazing number considering this was a relatively sparsely populated area – crowded the hills west of the Rock so as to get a grandstand view of the attack from a totally safe distance. Of course, many had come great distances, some from as far as France. Meanwhile, days in the Spanish and French camp were spent making courtesy calls and greeting some of the nobility that had come down from Paris and Madrid to see the event and, in some cases, participate as combatants. Still, no one could tell when exactly the attack would take place.

But it would be sooner than later. On or about 11 September, the Spanish even built a grandstand with some booths, all nicely decorated with red bunting, on the shore in front of the allied camp. It was undoubtedly intended for the senior officials and their companions so that they could watch the attack and capture of Gibraltar in comfort.

Within Gibraltar, everyone also knew that a major attack by the floating batteries was imminent. It might come just by sea or might even be a concerted sea and land attack, with thousands of troops making a gallant rush over the Neutral Grounds. Allied troop movements could be seen and there seemed to be more people than ever crowding the hills. The fire of the Spanish batteries was mainly directed at the Landport and its area. A night attack was not excluded and Governor Eliott had more fires lit that night as well as guard parties reinforced. Sure enough, at about ten in the evening, movement in the evening darkness was detected by sentries at Forbes's Barrier. When they challenged, the palisades forming the British outer line started going up in flames, lit by the lurking Spaniards, while the Spanish bombardment intensified. Around midnight, the Spanish gunboats closed in and fired at the Waterport. But, at two in the morning, the shooting abated and both sides retired to rest for what was left of the night.

The next day, 12 September, the garrison was a bit nervous and, at seven in the morning, a large number of sails were seen in the distance. The faint hope of a relief fleet gave way to grave thoughts: it was the combined fleet of Spain and France coming into the bay under the command of Admiral de Cordova seconded by ten Spanish and French admirals. The allied fleet now mustered 47 ships-of-the-line, including seven three-deckers, plus five bomb ketches, three frigates, a number of smaller vessels and support ships, the ten floating batteries and the small Spanish gunboats that were always at Algeciras. Nearly 300 boats to carry

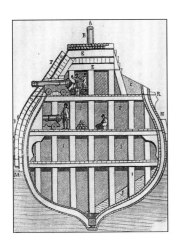

Floating battery profile plan, 1782. This plan concerns the larger, two-tiered vessels such as the flagship *Pastora* or the *Talla Piedra* that each had 31 guns and a crew of 760 men. These were ships that had been transformed for the purpose. The batteries were protected by extra layers of planking ('D') and the roof was also armoured ('E'). Ballast was deposited on the opposite side ('J') to compensate for the weight of the guns and armour. (From Conde de Clonard's *Historia organica* ... Author's photo)

troops had been constructed. With the arrival of the combined fleet at Algeciras, the naval superiority of the Spanish and French was overwhelming and the planned attack could now proceed.

A BITTER COUNCIL MEETING

That night, there was a tense meeting of the senior allied officers around a council table. The three main protagonists were Mshl de Crillon, R Adm Moreno and Col D'Arçon. There was considerable disagreement over the timing of the attack. Mshl de Crillon wanted to proceed at once, otherwise the whole operation would be seen as ridiculous. He had already re-scheduled it twice and was not anxious to incur the wrath of the tens of thousands who had come to watch the attack. Should there be many more days of delays, these disappointed spectators could spread very bad opinions about the way the siege was conducted. Another factor was that it was already mid-September and the season of storms and bad weather would soon arrive.

Col D'Arçon had far more practical arguments. His main concern was over the quality of the work done on the floating batteries. He had not been allowed to test them first and, even without a sea trial, serious problems mostly due to indifferent workmanship were appearing. If the 'battering ships' were to stand the fire from the batteries in Gibraltar, the caulking of the hulls – which had been badly put in – would have to be re-done. Related to this was a problem with the water pumps, which were faulty. If the caulking gave way, the floating batteries might take on too much water and sink, especially as they were quite heavy. The water pumps needed to be in top working order, not only because of the faulty caulking, but to extinguish fires that might be started on board by the British red-hot shots.

Admiral Moreno was not impressed by the workmanship on the floating batteries and worried about risking the lives of his sailors and gunners on board what seemed to be dubious vessels. However, he knew that Marshal de Crillon was critical of the recent lack of performance by his ships-of-the-line and was consequently somewhat sulky. He thought that it would be safer to delay and do the work, as D'Arçon suggested, so as to have good vessels for such an attack. Other problems such as the Spanish batteries failing to enfilade Gibraltar's lower batteries would also need time to be fixed.

Faced with such opinions, Marshal de Crillon became adamant and stood up to forcefully to make his point: the attack would absolutely proceed the next day! The time was right, he insisted, especially as it was rumoured that yet another large British fleet was on its way to supply and reinforce Gibraltar. The order was to attack.

D'Arçon despaired but knew he had to comply. Adm Moreno hinted that he might not undertake the attack. Mshl de Crillon reminded him that it was an order and that, not only would he dismiss Moreno if he did not attack, but also that he would dishonour him for not leading the floating batteries into combat. The die was cast. The attack would take place the next day.

Both Moreno and D'Arçon walked out of Mshl de Crillon's quarters quite bitter. The proud Spanish sea officer headed directly to the battering ship *Pastora*, his flagship, fuming and speaking to no one. The French engineer went to his tent to plan targets for the artillery and then, under the cover of darkness in a small rowboat, went within a thousand metres of Gibraltar's Old Mole to make soundings of the sand bars in the area to be attacked. Back in his quarters, he was still up with his charts at two in the morning when an orderly told him that the *Pastora* was about to sail. D'Arçon hurried to the docks, finding the place in much confusion as the ships were preparing to heave off. He boarded the *Tella Piedra*, commanded by a fellow countryman, the Prince de Nassau.

SAILING TO ATTACK

The ten battering ships under the command of R Adm Buenaventura Moreno consisted of:

Ship	Guns in use	Guns in reserve	Men	Commanders
Pastora	21	10	760	Buen.-Moreno
Talla Piedra	21	10	760	Prince de Nassau
Paula Prima	21	10	760	Langara
El Rosario	19	10	700	Muños
San Christobal	18	10	650	Gravina
Principe Carlos	11	4	400	Basorta
San Juan	9	4	340	Angeler
Paula Seconda	9	4	340	De Cosa
Santa Anna	7	4	300	Giocachea
Los Dolores	6	4	250	Sánchez

The list given in various accounts varies on some details but all agreed that it was an awesome little fleet packing extraordinary firepower. Its ships had 212 guns manned by some 5,260 officers and men. All the guns were of brass, which was of lighter weight and said to stand constant firings better. Whatever the forebodings of their commander and of the

The northern end of the Rock as seen from the west in 1782. This perspective view was essentially what the Spanish and French sailors and soldiers on the floating batteries saw as they approached on 13 September 1782. At water level, the Old Mole, Grand, Montague and Orange bastions punctuate the line wall. Further up, the Moorish castle and, a bit further up to its left, Willis's batteries at the edge of the steep cliff. Roads lead further up to Ince's Gallery (invisible). (Ink wash by J. Reinhart. Museo Naval, Madrid. Author's photo)

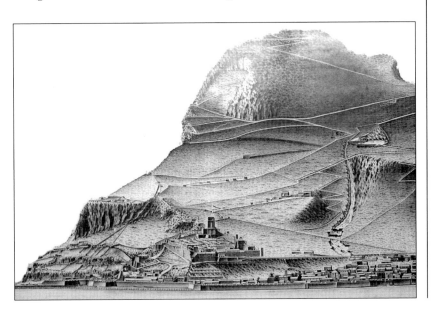

chief engineer, the officers and men were motivated and confident that they would bring Gibraltar to its knees at last.

As it turned out, R Adm Moreno had second thoughts about sailing in the dark of the night into totally uncharted waters. His slow-moving ships might run aground on the Rock and even be captured by the ever-vigilant British garrison. He therefore waited until daylight to issue sailing orders. It was a fine day with a north-westerly breeze that slowly carried the battering ships out of Algeciras. On the shore, excitement mounted as it provided a fine spectacle for the officials, who included Louis XVI's brother the Comte d'Artois, now taking their seats in the grandstand while tens of thousands watched from the hills.

In Gibraltar, too, the spectacle drew attention and everyone was watching what the movements of these curious-looking ships would be. Perhaps they were taking them out on their trial sailing run, certainly the most logical thing. On the other hand, the British could see a great deal of animation on the enemy shore and on the hills and the grandstand was full. Governor Eliott took a quick ride to see for himself. Taking no chances, he mustered the artillerymen to their guns and, at eight in the morning, ordered that the grates be lit for red-hot shots.

The floating batteries deployed in the bay, in line with Fort San Felipe at the western end of the Spanish line, and supposedly fireproof and unsinkable, they approached their objective: the west walls and batteries of Gibraltar. From the grandstand, the floating batteries with their thickly armoured hulls seemed invincible. Outside sprinklers were working, which made their sides gleam in the morning sun, and their flags and banners flew in the wind. It was a grand sight. Yet, to the informed officers on the French staff, things were already not going according to plan by nine in the morning. The two lead ships, the *Pastora* and the *Talla Piedra*, were going further and further ahead, much in advance of the other eight battering ships. Furthermore, neither Adm de Cordova's ships-of-the-line nor Adm Barcelo's light vessels looked as if they would sail to support the battering ships.

By 9.30, the *Pastora* and the *Talla Piedra* were moving opposite the King's Bastion and anchored at a distance of about 1,000 metres. They

The town of Gibraltar seen from the west in 1782. The King's Bastion is to the left on the waterfront, at the right the South Bastion and to the very left the Ragged Staff, which marks the southern end of the town. The 'Moorish wall' goes up the Rock. (Ink wash by J. Reinhart. Museo Naval, Madrid. Author's photo)

were followed by the other floating batteries. The *Los Dolores, San Christobál, Príncipe Carlos* and *Paula Secunda* anchored at the sandbank at about 1,200 metres from the Old Mole; the *Santa Anna* was between them and the *Pastora*, the three others being further back and to the south. All now had their batteries pointing towards Gibraltar's west walls and batteries, which mounted about 150 pieces of artillery.

The most exposed and closest in range of the floating batteries were the *Pastora* and the *Talla Piedra*; the British gunners made them their main targets for nearly two hours. In the grandstand, French and Spanish staff officers worried as the deployment of the floating batteries was not going according to plan. There should have been more in front of the Old Mole to pulverize the place with the help of the Spanish land batteries. But the four floating batteries at the sandbank were farther away and their fire could not be as efficient. Thus, the Old Mole stood up to it quite well. The other floating batteries, although individually quite formidable, were too spread out. Perhaps R Adm Moreno should have been trying to correct the alignment but this was now almost impossible to do and he had more immediate worries, his ship being a prime target for the British artillerymen.

Meanwhile, behind Gibraltar's walls, the British watched with some admiration the admittedly difficult and dangerous manoeuvre of the floating batteries moving into bombardment range of the walls, especially as it was done unsupported from the rest of the fleet:

> By a quarter before ten, wrote Governor Eliott in his report to the Earl of Shelburne, they were anchored in line, at a distance of a thousand to twelve hundred yards; immediately a heavy cannonade began from all the ships, supported by the cannon, and mortars in the enemy lines, and approaches. At the same moment, our batteries opened (CO 91/29).

The British gunners could only fire with 'cold shot' as the grates and ovens had not yet heated up enough to supply red-hot shot. Governor

The attack of the floating batteries on 13 September 1782, as seen from slightly up on the Rock. On the left foreground, the King's Bastion battles with the floating batteries as do other batteries up to the Old Mole further north. The town is in ruins from the Spanish bombardments. This print by R.W. Patten is one of the most accurate showing the event. (Anne S.K. Brown Military Collection, Brown University, Providence, USA. Author's photo)

The attack of 13 September 1782 seen from the south. The floating batteries, shown in a somewhat too perfect line, are hotly engaged by guns at the end of the Ragged Staff (a crooked jetty) and along the town's line wall and batteries. (Plate from Spilsbury's journal. Author's photo)

Eliott was present at the King's Bastion and, with his men, was dismayed to see that the cannon balls and shells just bounced off the thick walls and roofs of what seemed to be indestructible ships. The only solution seemed to reside in as much red-hot shot as possible and the governor called on the artificers to supply this in quantity as soon as possible. The desperate artificers could do little to raise the temperature of the embers but, not having enough grates, they used the corners of destroyed houses near the Line Wall batteries as makeshift ovens. Cannon balls were put in corners with burning coals and wood piled on top. But it would be hours before red-hot shot could be delivered.

While the main shooting match was between the two floating batteries and the King's Bastion on the morning of 13 September, the bombardment from over 200 heavy-calibre Spanish guns, mortars and howitzers from their land batteries caused some damage and casualties on the north side. The fire from the other floating batteries was not too effective so far. But the two most exposed floating batteries showed no sign of having suffered much damage apart from their riggings being shot away. Their armour was holding up, although Col Boyd noted one lucky shot that went through a porthole and presumably caused damage and injuries inside. The fire from these two floating batteries was not causing much damage either to the sturdy King's Bastion and its adjoining walls. Indeed, Capt Spillbury noted that 'they fired a great deal into the water'. So far, the morning's bombardment was a draw as thick smoke covered the area in something of a haze.

RED-HOT SHOT

By noon, the artificers were delivering red-hot shot to the British gunners and Governor Eliott ordered them to be fired. As the cannons were constantly at a slight elevation, the red-hot shot did not need to be rammed in and, reaching the black powder charge previously put in, caused the charge to explode and propel the shot. This meant that rounds could be fired very fast. Soon, it almost rained red-hot shot on all the floating batteries. The British batteries were kept supplied by infantrymen from the 39th and 72nd regiments organized into supply crews between the grates and the guns. For all involved, the handling of red-hot shot at a rapid rate was gruelling and dangerous work but it was carried out with remarkable speed and success.

On the floating batteries, the change of ammunition by the British did not initially have much effect. True, the red-hot projectiles were more annoying. It was sometimes necessary for men to get out on the roof of their ship to douse or get rid of the red-hot balls that lodged there but, on the whole, the menace seemed minimal. On board the *Talla Piedra*, hope soared when some stones from the King's Bastions were knocked off and the Prince de Nassau even hoped to make a breach. He also signalled to the main fleet for reinforcements to replace some of the killed and wounded on board.

The British on the line walls and batteries were little affected by the fire of the floating batteries and, blackened by the black powder's smoke, fired their ordnance as fast as they could at their targets. This was made relatively easy as the enemy batteries were anchored. Once the range had been found, there was no need to reckon a precise aim – several shots in a short time would be fired instead of taking aim every time. Handling red-hot shot amidst smoke, in the vicinity of furnace-like grates and piles of flaming red-hot embers mixed with cannon balls under a hot sun, made the men very thirsty. Water was at times in short supply and some men carrying pails would go to fountains, ducking the enemy's shot, to get water. The men at the batteries and the west walls were relatively safe from enemy fire. Even in the King's Bastion, which was subject to the fire of two floating batteries, Governor Eliott and his men did not feel unduly threatened.

Further south, Gibraltar residents were quite safe from the enemy's fire and many watched the action from the walls or up the cliffs or from Rosia Bay. The ten Spanish floating batteries anchored northwards were in view amidst the smoke but there were no other enemy ships or gunboats deployed further south to challenge Parson's Battery or Europa Point, which could have been useful diversions as it would have strained Gibraltar's defences. Governor Eliott and his officers kept an eye out for such a move but, so far, the combined fleet and the gunboats across the bay were not sailing. The most dangerous area in Gibraltar was actually to

The British gun positions were given as much protection as possible by adding caissons of barrels, wood and earth to the embrasures. (Plate from Spilsbury's journal. Author's photo)

P. Courcelle

THE ATTACK OF THE FLOATING BATTERIES,
13 SEPTEMBER 1782 (pages 72–73)

The ten floating batteries (1) that were anchored off Gibraltar's western walls (2) were supposed to subdue the British fortifications, make a breach and provide the opportunity for the combined Spanish and French fleet (3) to land contingents on the peninsula that would overcome the British garrison. But many things went wrong with this plan. The floating batteries were not anchored quite at the planned spots and could not move. Seeing this, the combined fleet commander did not move his ships closer, so the floating batteries ended up being immobile and without support. For their part, the British gunners were extremely active and proficient, notably in firing red-hot shot at the floating batteries in great numbers during the afternoon and evening. The action is shown in the late afternoon/early evening. There is smoke in the area of the floating batteries from the tremendous cannon fire, but also, by this time, from fires that are starting to be apparent in the *Pastora* and the *Talla Piedra* (4). The design of the five larger floating batteries with two gun decks is shown as seen from the front at the left of the plate (5). It is based on watercolours showing the design of these vessels by Lt Koelher of the Royal Artillery, who was present during the attack, now preserved in the Public Records Office. There was also considerable smoke with some conflagrations in Gibraltar (6) due to intense firings being returned by the British gunners as well as from the Spanish bombardments from both the floating batteries and the land batteries to the north (7). In spite of all the cannon balls and bombs shot at them, damage to Gibraltar's fortifications was relatively minor while the floating batteries were increasingly looking to be in serious trouble. By then Governor Eliott and his men knew they had repulsed one of the most formidable attacks in the annals of siege warfare. (Patrice Courcelle)

the north, in the area of the Grand Parade. There, the bombardment from the Spanish land batteries continued to be very intense and soldiers were constantly trying to get out of the way or scramble for cover when a shell's hissing was heard.

As the afternoon wore on, the confident mood of the Spanish and French onlookers became more sombre. The floating batteries were seen to be totally immobilized off Gibraltar's coast and within range of the enemy's batteries. They could not move and, indeed, the Prince de Nassau's *Talla Piedra* had touched bottom. Staff officers around Marshal de Crillon were muttering. Obviously the proper soundings of the seabed had not been made, or else had been very badly sounded by the Spanish Navy. Anchors with cables should have been deposited in the area previous to the attack so that the floating batteries could have hauled themselves out of danger. Worst of all, the planned disposition of the floating batteries, which aimed at levelling the Old Mole area and making a breach there, was much too spread out. The soundings, the anchors, the dispositions, all this was the responsibility of R Adm Moreno and it had all gone wrong with no possibility of being corrected. Moreno's only saving grace was that he was in the heat of the action on board the *Pastora*. On the other hand, the floating batteries, considered faulty by Col D'Arçon the night before, were holding up remarkably well. They did indeed seem unsinkable and fireproof.

THE COMBINED FLEET'S INACTION

From across the bay at Algeciras, there was no movement to send reinforcements and supplies to the floating batteries, and to take out the wounded. Adm de Cordova, a man the French suspected to be a master at avoiding action and qualified as 'nul' (nil) by Mshl de Crillon's son, who surely echoed his father's opinion, chose to be prudent and take no risks. As the supreme naval commander, a positive order on his part in the early afternoon such as creating a diversion and reinforcing the batteries would have had every chance of lessening the impending disaster looming over the immobile floating batteries. By doing nothing, he sealed the fate of the brave men in the floating batteries.

His inaction was not necessarily shared by his officers. The usually aggressive V Adm Barcelo was doubly upset to see his comrades being shot at with no relief as he watched the action on his deck, and he must have damned those in charge for having given command of the fleet to de Cordova rather than to him. As it was, he had been superseded. He was bitter and, as his admiral would do nothing, the only thing left was to fume. Another worthy Spanish fleet officer was Capt José de Mazarredo, destined to become one of Spain's best admirals. He was de Cordova's chief-of-staff and had planned his one successful action, the capture of a huge British convoy two years earlier. The present lack of action must have turned his blood along with that of many onlookers in the fleet.

Marshal de Crillon's actions during the afternoon and early evening also seem to have had an air of *laisser faire*. It had been planned that Adm de Cordova would move his ships in support of the floating batteries at one point of the engagement but this was the naval commander's prerogative. Mshl de Crillon had already ordered the attack over R Adm

ATTACK OF THE FLOATING BATTERIES, 13 SEPTEMBER 1782

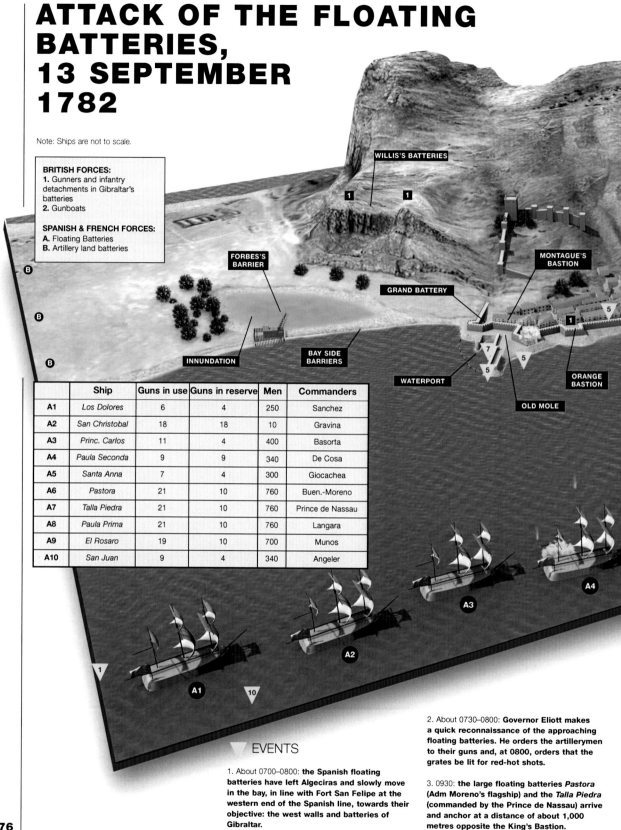

Note: Ships are not to scale.

BRITISH FORCES:
1. Gunners and infantry detachments in Gibraltar's batteries
2. Gunboats

SPANISH & FRENCH FORCES:
A. Floating Batteries
B. Artillery land batteries

WILLIS'S BATTERIES

FORBES'S BARRIER

MONTAGUE'S BASTION

GRAND BATTERY

INNUNDATION

BAY SIDE BARRIERS

WATERPORT

ORANGE BASTION

OLD MOLE

	Ship	Guns in use	Guns in reserve	Men	Commanders
A1	Los Dolores	6	4	250	Sanchez
A2	San Christobal	18	18	10	Gravina
A3	Princ. Carlos	11	4	400	Basorta
A4	Paula Seconda	9	9	340	De Cosa
A5	Santa Anna	7	4	300	Giocachea
A6	Pastora	21	10	760	Buen.-Moreno
A7	Talla Piedra	21	10	760	Prince de Nassau
A8	Paula Prima	21	10	760	Langara
A9	El Rosaro	19	10	700	Munos
A10	San Juan	9	4	340	Angeler

EVENTS

1. About 0700–0800: **the Spanish floating batteries have left Algeciras and slowly move in the bay, in line with Fort San Felipe at the western end of the Spanish line, towards their objective: the west walls and batteries of Gibraltar.**

2. About 0730–0800: **Governor Eliott makes a quick reconnaissance of the approaching floating batteries. He orders the artillerymen to their guns and, at 0800, orders that the grates be lit for red-hot shots.**

3. 0930: **the large floating batteries Pastora (Adm Moreno's flagship) and the Talla Piedra (commanded by the Prince de Nassau) arrive and anchor at a distance of about 1,000 metres opposite the King's Bastion.**

To the British behind the walls of Gibraltar, the formidable floating batteries they saw coming at them on the morning of 13 September was the signal that the decisive battle had come. But the British garrison, although impressed at the sight of these seemingly indestructible boats, was not about to give up without a very stiff fight. A fierce artillery duel ensued to settle Gibraltar's fate.

GRAND PARADE

KING'S BASTION

c. 1,000 m

4. 0930–0945: **the other floating batteries arrive on the scene opposite Gibraltar's western walls. The *Los Dolores*, *San Christobal*, *Principe Carlos* and *Paula Secunda* anchored at the sandbank at about 1,200 metres from the Old Mole, the *Santa Anna* is between them and the *Pastora*, the three others are further back and to the south. The disposition of the floating batteries is somewhat further north than planned by Col D'Arçon.**

5. 0945: **both the floating batteries and the land batteries at the isthmus open a heavy fire. Governor Eliott orders his gunners to open fire on the floating batteries. There is no sign of Adm de Cordova's combined fleet coming out of Algeciras to join the floating batteries.**

6. 0945–1200: **the Spanish floating batteries do not inflict much damage on Gibraltar's fortifications and the British gunners find that the floating batteries do not suffer much damage apart from their riggings shot away. The British are using 'cold shot' as the grates and makeshift ovens are not yet hot enough to supply red-hot shot.**

7. 1200 and into the afternoon: **the British artificers start to deliver red-hot shot to the gunners. This does not seem, initially, to damage the Spanish floating batteries.**

8. **Through the day, Gibraltar's Grand Parade is very heavily bombarded by the batteries at the isthmus and is considered the most dangerous place on the Rock.**

9. About 1700–1715: **fire is discovered on board the *Talla Piedra*. The Prince de Nassau orders the powder barrels doused with water before the flames get to them. The *Talla Piedra* ceases fire. At about 1800, the *Pastora* is also on fire. The other vessels continue their fire but the 'Grand Attack' has failed.**

10. **At about midnight, Adm de Cordova orders the remaining floating batteries to be abandoned and set on fire. Boats from Algeciras try to rescue their crews. Bombardment from the Spanish land batteries continues. The British think the attack might not be over and wonder about the Spanish and French small boats that have come to the floating batteries.**

11. **At about 0300 on 14 September, a squadron of 12 British gunboats led by Sir Roger Curtis set out from the New Mole and attack the Spanish and French boats who beat a retreat. The British sailors then see that many men are still stranded on the floating batteries and they try to save them.**

12. **At about 0500, a floating battery explodes followed by another somewhat later. The British suffer some casualties due to explosions and their gunboats go back to Gibraltar with the Spanish and French sailors they managed to rescue. At about 0800, the Spanish land batteries routinely open fire. The British gunboats still trying to rescue sailors must withdraw as a result. Fire eventually ceases but it is too late. All the floating batteries are destroyed by fire during 14 September.**

77

Moreno's and Col D'Arçon's bitter opposition and this attack was not going as well as planned. To order Adm de Cordova to join in the fray would certainly have resulted in a huge dispute among the allied staff, possibly a division between the French and the Spanish officers, with the proud Spaniards openly contesting the authority of the French marshal. With an ally that was very sensitive on the 'points of honour' regarding national pride, Mshl de Crillon had to consider diplomatic issues as carefully as military objectives. So, perhaps, nothing further could be done. On board the floating batteries, meanwhile, officers and men had the increasing feeling that they had been totally abandoned to their fate. When a fellow officer on the *Talla Piedra* queried when help would come, an angry D'Arçon answered, 'Can't you see, my friend, that we are abandoned by God and by men?'

Within Gibraltar, the only concern everyone had was to see if the floating batteries would ever sustain serious damage. By late afternoon, in spite of all the red-hot shots fired, this was still not in clear evidence amidst all the smoke. Of all the British batteries, the King's Bastion was the most formidable and its fire concentrated mainly on the *Pastora* and the *Talla Piedra*. On board the floating batteries, the gunners frantically worked their guns, blackened by the powder and choking in the smoke-filled gun decks. They seemed invulnerable but, at around five in the afternoon, sailors on board the *Talla Piedra* spotted thick smoke coming from below. Something was wrong. What they found there was a glowing fire set by a red-hot shot that had penetrated through the hull and sand to lodge itself in the timbers. Ironically, it had broken through one of the faulty water pipes, which was dry. The shot had probably been there for some hours slowly burning into the wood but only when it had more air did flames start to appear. Col D'Arçon had a look and was convinced that, with more air, the whole ship would be engulfed by fire. Apprised of the impending disaster, the Prince de Nassau ordered the powder barrels doused with water before the flames got to them. On shore, the British could now see smoke coming from the vessel and men coming out to fill water buckets. On board, D'Arçon, de Nassau and Capt Juan Mendoza, the Spanish commander, quickly concluded that they were doomed. There was no way they could take their vessel out of action, especially as its rigging had been shot away, which also made distress signals impossible. The *Talla Piedra* ceased firing.

The Spanish shore batteries had also ceased their intense bombardment a little earlier. The reason was simple enough: the Spanish gunners had run out of powder and shot. By then, it was clear that the attack was not going well and no further ammunition was sent, or orders to the exhausted and disappointed artillerymen to resume shooting.

In the bay, the other most targeted floating battery, R Adm Moreno's *Pastora*, had been seen by Governor Eliott at two in the afternoon 'to smoke, as if on fire, and [had] a few men up on the roof, searching for the cause' but it must have been a false alarm. By about six, it now also started to show the effects of the red-hot shot. Several small fires were spotted as increasing amounts of smoke emerged from the ship's hull. Measures were taken on board to control the fires and the ship continued shooting.

In Algeciras, the French admiral, the Comte de Guichen, and his officers found the predicament of the floating batteries intolerable. But the French squadron could not move unless Admiral de Cordova ordered it and no orders were forthcoming. At about six, seeing the smoke coming out of the *Pastora* and the *Talla Piedra*, Adm de Guichen sent a boat to the *Pastora* offering the assistance of the French ships. R Adm Moreno replied with bitter sarcasm that everything had gone according to plan so no help was necessary. It was a slap in the face to the allied senior commanders. By seven, fire was gaining ground, the *Pastora* ceased firing, and Moreno sent a message to Mshl de Crillon requesting help to save his men. By then, Governor Eliott noted, the floating batteries only 'fired from a few guns, and that, only at intervals'.

The marshal and his staff had been watching the whole operation collapse during the afternoon but knew there was hardly anything land forces could do. Adm de Cordova's inaction ensured failure but, at about eight in the evening, Mshl de Crillon sent a message to the admiral praying him to sail and try to save the men on the floating batteries. The admiral had at his disposal some 47 ships-of-the-line within the range of two cannon shots from the scene of the action. Yet again, de Cordova would do nothing and argued that the wind was not blowing the right way – it was as if he had never sailed against the wind!

Long before then, the situation had become desperate on the floating batteries. The Prince de Nassau had left the *Talla Piedra* to seek help and V Adm Moreno was about to quit the *Pastora*. The other eight vessels had been battered, too, but, being further out, did not seem as badly damaged. They were nevertheless immobile like rocks in the water and had ceased firing.

In Gibraltar, the mood went from guarded optimism to joy. By six in the evening, Governor Eliott and his men knew they had beaten a rather extraordinary attack. The question remained if another attack might not be made. There still were over 50 Spanish and French warships within sight and up to 35,000 allied troops camped outside (Governor Eliott believed there were 40,000). Two floating batteries were on fire but the other eight seemed relatively unscathed. The British gunners therefore continued to fire at them and their fire was returned. The artillerymen were now very tired and were replaced in part by sailors. Governor Eliott wanted them to be relatively rested for the next day as the enemy fleet might attack to support the remaining floating batteries. What the British in Gibraltar could not know at the time was the effect of their victory on the morale of their opponents.

The wily Mshl de Crillon understood this a lot better, his command being very much tied to Spanish and French politics. Indeed, the day before the attack, he had sent a courier to Madrid to publish a letter in which he expressed publicly his doubts concerning the use of floating batteries. Thus, if the attack failed, Col D'Arçon would be the scapegoat, or so he thought. In the meantime, the best thing to do was to wait for the outcome. In the meantime, the Prince de Nassau had arrived at the marshal's headquarters and described an increasingly desperate situation. At about half past ten, the prince and the marshal went to see Adm de Cordova and asked him to detach some frigates from his fleet to rescue the stranded men and even drag back those floating batteries that seemed intact. A council was called and Adm de Cordova flatly refused to risk any of his ships in such a mission; the battle was already lost and there was no point to losing even more ships and men. His cold logic was certainly correct. With that, there was only one course of action left: to send out

View on the morning of 14 September 1782, following the Grand Attack of the previous day. One of the attacking floating batteries is on fire and another explodes producing a large mushroom-shaped cloud. More of the ships were actually on fire at the time. This contemporary print, apparently based on a view and maps in Drinkwater's book, gives a good general view of the Rock from the Spanish lines at La Línea. Approaching it from this narrow peninsula would have been near suicidal. Every tier of the Rock had British batteries and the small gun ports of Ince's gallery can also be faintly seen. At sea level, the guns of the Grand Battery and the Old Mole, extending into the bay (at right) could sweep the flat grounds between the small lake-like 'inundations'. (Anne S.K. Brown Military Collection, Brown University, Providence, USA. Author's photo)

small craft to rescue what men they could and to set fire to the remaining floating batteries so the British would not capture them. The officers going out in the longboats were to instruct the captains of the stranded floating batteries to set fire to those vessels not already in flames.

It was now later in the evening and darkness had come to the area. But there were many lights in the area from the numerous ships in the harbour as well as the countless campfires in the army camp and on the hills. There were up to 145,000 people – the army of 40,000, some 30,000 sailors in the combined fleet and the estimated 80,000 spectators on the hills – watching what would happen next in the bay. Cannon flashes could still be seen from Gibraltar. Two floating batteries were burning. Rockets went up from the other floating batteries; these were distress signals by their increasingly desperate crews who wanted to be rescued by their fleet. At 'about midnight,' Capt Spillbury wrote, both sides 'ceased firing'.

THE RESCUE ATTEMPTS

Sometime after midnight, launches and various types of small boats from the combined fleet at Algeciras were finally arriving on the scene 'to take out the men on board the burning ships'. Governor Eliott now noted that 'many shots were still fired from those [floating batteries] in which the flames had yet made no considerable progress; and the fire from the enemy's batteries on shore did not in the least diminish'. Thus, the bombardment of Gibraltar, after a pause in the evening, continued into the night. All this may have been done to provide cover for the Spanish and French boats while they were near the floating batteries. Unfortunately for the stranded men, the bombardment had dire consequences.

At about one in the morning, the scene lit up considerably as the *Pastora* was engulfed by flames from stem to stern, then the *Talla Piedra* and flames started to engulf four other floating batteries in the following hours. These new fires were not because of the British red-hot shot, as Governor Eliott and other British participants believed, but the result of the orders to burn the vessels. Indeed, some captains refused, at least initially, to carry out the order but eventually relented when they accepted there was no alternative. The bay was lit up almost as if it were daylight and the many Spanish boats coming over could be seen from the walls of Gibraltar.

To the British in Gibraltar, the enemy's cannon balls and shells signalled that it was 'back to a normal day' on the Rock. The boats seen

to be lurking about the floating batteries were certainly reminiscent of, and indeed sometimes the same, gunboats that almost nightly came close to fire shots on the town during past years. Except that, on this occasion, there were many more boats of all sorts.

At two in the morning, the squadron of 12 British gunboats with about 250 men on board under the command of Capt Sir Roger Curtis left the New Mole and headed north to the area of the floating batteries, which was reached an hour later. They now 'formed a line upon the enemy's flank, advancing and firing with great order and expedition, which so astonished and disconcerted the enemy, [that] they fled precipitately with all their boats, abandoning the ships in which some officers and many of their men, including some wounded, were left to perish', reported Governor Eliott. On the scene, Capt Curtis and his men now discovered from prisoners that there were still many men on board the burning floating batteries and, indeed, could hear their desperate cries for help. The whole operation was now transformed into a rescue attempt to rescue fellow sailors. It was now about four in the morning and eight floating batteries were burning, keeping the bay lit up. Governor Eliott, still in the King's Bastion, had ordered his gunners to cease fire while Sir Roger's gunboats were out and, as the first tinges of dawn appeared, could see the British boats amongst the flaming vessels, trying to take men on board, some of whom still refused to be rescued by their enemy. Then, a disaster struck.

At about five in the morning, the flames reached the powder magazine in one of the floating batteries and it blew up in a tremendous explosion that made a huge noise and produced a mushroom-like cloud of smoke. The British boats were still amongst the vessels in flames and many Spaniards now changed their mind and tried to get on board the British boats. In some cases, British sailors even boarded the burning hulks to carry men off and, on board the *Pastora*, found Spain's royal standard, which they took with them. It was later hung from a gun on the King's Battery. Then another floating battery blew up in another huge explosion. This time, a nearby British boat was sunk and the coxswain of Sir Roger's gunboat was killed with a sailor wounded and the boat's bottom pierced by falling debris. It was getting much too dangerous to

Following the defeat of the attack of 13 September 1782, British boats from Gibraltar went out, often at great peril, to try to save the Spanish and French survivors of the doomed floating batteries. Capt Curtis wrote to the Lords of the Admiralty: 'The scene at this time before me was dreadful to a high degree; numbers of men crying from amidst the flames, some upon pieces of wood in the water, others appearing in the ships where the fire had as yet made but little progress, all expressing by speech and gesture the deepest distress, and all imploring assistance, formed a spectacle of horror not easily to be described. Every exertion was made to relieve them; and I have inexpressible happiness in informing my lords, that the number saved amounts to 13 officers and 344 men. One officer and 29 wounded (some of them dreadfully) taken from among the slain in the holds, are in our hospital, and many of them in a fair way.' (Print after James Jefferies. Anne S.K. Brown Military Collection, Brown University, Providence, USA. Author's photo)

try to rescue any more and Capt Curtis ordered the flotilla to withdraw. As if the explosions were not enough to hinder rescue attempts, the Spanish batteries at the isthmus now opened fire. The British sailors nevertheless took men off two other vessels before retiring.

The opening up of the Spanish batteries on Gibraltar at their usual hour, eight in the morning, was an incredibly stupid act. All the British were doing at that point was trying to rescue men from the burning floating batteries. It was a tragic mistake in that no one appears to have given orders not to fire at the usual appointed hour that morning. The result was dramatic and certainly spelt the doom of many a brave man to a horrible death by fire. Very few men could swim in those days; none made it to shore that way, and very few hanging on to floating debris. In the Spanish lines, an officer at last realized the folly of shooting at those who were trying to save their comrades from certain death and the firing ceased. But it was too late and the harm had been done.

Nevertheless, the British gunboats had managed to rescue many men and the number of captured personnel came to 357 officers and men. Some were wounded or burned and they were sent to the hospital. The others went to a camp on Windmill Hill. The captured officers were put in the care of the garrison's officers who tried to give them some comfort. It is said that when they saw the furnaces with red-hot shot, they made a discouraged shrug and looked back at their burning vessels.

The worse was yet to come. There were still men on board the floating batteries. Two had blown up but six were still burning and two had not caught fire. Through the smoke, men could be seen on top, wildly gesticulating though the flames. It was a horrible sight but nothing could be done due to the risk of explosions. Between nine and eleven, three more vessels blew up and a fourth burned down to water level, as had the *Pastora* and the *Talla Piedra* earlier. This left the two vessels to the north that were not on fire. A Spanish felucca approached one of them, probably to set it on fire and take on survivors, but was driven off by the British gunners as it was a potential prize. They were to be disappointed. At about noon, it erupted into flames and blew up shortly thereafter. The last floating battery was stuck tilted on a sandbank with debris and dead bodies floating about. Capt Gibson went to see if it could be salvaged but, finding it could not, set it on fire and the last floating battery was consumed during the afternoon of 14 September 1782. Thus ended the Grand Attack.

Explosion of a floating battery causing a large and impressive mushroom of smoke with debris falling all around. (Plate by Capt Spilsbury, who was present, from his journal. Author's photo)

Besides the officers and men captured by the British, the Spanish and French lost 1,473 killed, wounded or missing. The British had 15 killed (including one Royal Artillery officer) and 68 wounded (including five officers). Half of these were from the Royal Artillery, which was the unit most heavily involved in this action. General Boyd rightly wrote of the gunners that 'Braver soldiers and better practices from the Batteries in the Universe was never made than what has crown'd this day.'

Governor Eliott and all his men had gained an outstanding victory. Not only had the much-vaunted unsinkable floating batteries been repulsed, they had been entirely destroyed. On the side of the allies, utter discouragement set in, as it was indeed a bitter blow to all their plans and hopes. For months and years to come, accusations and recriminations flew, especially between Col D'Arçon and Mshl Crillon, while everyone felt somewhat disgraced. French wits, looking for some humour through it all, coined a joke to the effect that 'this time, it was not the wooden horse that had taken Troy, but it was Troy that had burned the wooden horse.'

The Duc de Crillon as depicted in a c. 1782 British cartoon of the period, trying to encourage his somewhat hesitant Spanish allies to attack Gibraltar, even as a shower of bombs and cannon balls from the Rock is fired at the allied besiegers. (Anne S.K. Brown Military Collection, Brown University, Providence, USA. Author's photo)

ADMIRAL HOWE'S RELIEF

Adm Lord Howe led the fleet that provided the final relief of Gibraltar in October 1782. This was done by skilfully outmanoeuvring the combined Spanish and French squadrons led by Adm de Cordova that were suppose to blockade Gibraltar. Howe's flagship was HMS *Victory*. (Author's photo)

Once the emotions and elations of the Grand Attack were over, everyone realized that the Great Siege was still on. The destruction of the floating batteries might have been a great success but there were still a large number of troops outside Gibraltar and a very large fleet anchored at Algeciras. The Spanish batteries on the isthmus continued their relentless fire while Governor Eliott and his officers prepared for a possible attack. By the end of September, it was clear that another Grand Attack would not be made but the annoying night forays of the Spanish gunboats continued.

In the Hispano-French camp, the notion of starving out the garrison of Gibraltar was the priority, especially as there was now Adm de Cordova's large combined fleet of 44 ships-of-the-line in the bay. However, both sides knew that a large relief fleet under the command of Adm Richard, Lord Howe had sailed from England and its fate might decide that of Gibraltar.

Lord Howe's 34 ships-of-the-line, escorting 31 transport ships, reached the area in mid-October. The ever-cautious Adm de Cordova sailed out to meet him. After several days of a cat-and-mouse game in the straits, de Cordova was out-sailed by Lord Howe and the transport ships came into Gibraltar. They were full of supplies and food and also brought the 25th and 59th regiments to reinforce the garrison, which now exceeded 7,000 men. The Rock was again supplied with food and ammunition to hold out.

The two fleets lurking in the Straits avoided combat and once his mission was accomplished, Lord Howe sailed back to England while Adm de Cordova took the combined allied fleet to Cadiz. It was now clear that Gibraltar was not likely to fall.

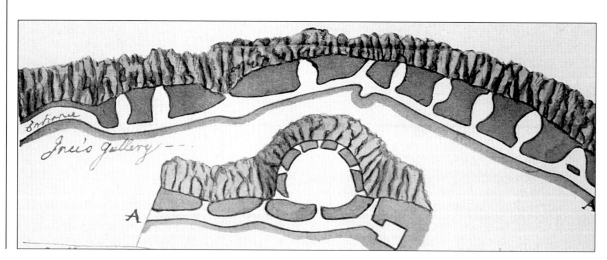

Spanish infantry grenadiers and fusiliers in camp. Between 1779 and 1783, the area outside Gibraltar saw mushrooming 'tent cities' to house the tens of thousands of troops posted there. This varied from about 14,000 in the autumn of 1779 to over 35,000 in September 1782. (Engraving after Geminez. Private collection. Author's photo)

Spanish artillery fire decreased to about 200 rounds a day by mid-November. Clearly, the defeat of the floating batteries and Lord Howe's convoy had ensured that Gibraltar would hold out for a very long time to come. Sir Roger Curtis had gone back to England with Lord Howe's fleet to convey the message that all was well at the Rock. On the Franco-Spanish side, they could only shrug their shoulders at the successive failures. Amidst rumours of negotiations for peace, there was nothing much to do except maintain a land blockade with bombardments and the occasional gunboat raids by night. The bay now had very few ships, the crowded hills of September were now deserted and, as weeks went by, the tent cities in the allied camp began to shrink as some troops departed.

Gibraltar nevertheless remained under pressure. On 25 December, the fourth Christmas of the Great Siege, the Spanish batteries and gunboats opened up an intense fire in the afternoon, causing a few casualties. On 1 January 1783, Governor Eliott celebrated New Year's Day in a ceremony around a Spanish gun with the Spanish flag over it taken on 13 September with the band playing 'God Save the King' for the benefit of allied ears. More gunboats came over to bombard four days later so Governor Eliott had red-hot shot fired into the Spanish camp from the Old Mole. All this had been punctuated by many messengers from Mshl de Crillon bearing flags of truce, seen as a duplicity that enraged Governor Eliott and the garrison. The Spanish were also trying to mine the base of the Rock in an attempt to destroy Ince's Gallery, which now had six gun embrasures, but Governor Eliott was not too concerned about this. Rather, the prospect of peace had spread some levity amongst officers and men in the garrison. On 19 January, the stern old governor made it known that there would be no more entertainment and that all duties and military behaviour were to be strictly observed. A few days later, a soldier of the 97th was executed for robbery.

OPPOSITE PAGE **Plan of Ince's Gallery carved into the Rock during 1782–83. At top is the corridor with nine small galleries leading to 'A', the large St George's Hall shown below. (Plate from Spilsbury's journal. Author's photo)**

THE GREAT SIEGE ENDS

On the morning of 2 February, a Spanish vessel flying a flag of truce approached and was met by a launch from Gibraltar. The Spanish sailors shouted '*Todos amigos*' – 'we are all friends'; they were bringing the news of a ceasefire. The next day, Spanish sentries in their forward works came out to chat with British sentries, but Governor Eliott had received no official notification from Mshl de Crillon and ordered guns fired over their head. On the 5th, Mshl de Crillon obliged and the British stopped their fire. After three years, seven months and 12 days, the Great Siege was over and Gibraltar had not fallen.

Nevertheless, the garrison's guard routines were kept up as before. The Spanish naval blockade was lifted and, on 5 March, a schooner arrived with gifts and congratulations from the wily Emperor of Morocco. However, Governor Eliott did not yet have any confirmation from Britain of the ceasefire so he was rather cautious. Finally, on 10 March, the frigate HMS *Thetis* came in with the official news that preliminaries for peace had indeed been signed. Sir Roger Curtis was on board bringing news of the cabinet, the thanks of the King and of Parliament to the garrison and the Order of the Bath for Governor Eliott.

It all had come at a price. From 1779 to 1783, the Gibraltar garrison's losses were:

Killed and dead of wounds: 333
Disabled by wounds: 138
Dead of sickness (except scurvy): 536
Discharged from sickness: 181
Deserted: 43

For a grand total of 1,231 officers, NCOs and private soldiers. Estimated deaths from scurvy came to about 500. Deaths due to sickness had been much higher, over a thousand, compared to 333 due to enemy fire. Of the 1,010 wounded, 872 recovered fully. For the British, the losses had been quite limited.

For the Spanish and French, the exact figures remain uncertain but the casualties were naturally much higher. A British spy reported 3,752 killed and missing from 1779 to 4 November 1782, a high but credible figure as the Spanish and French were much more exposed in their lines and floating batteries (CO 91/29).

On 12 March, Mshl de Crillon and Governor Eliott met and, in the days ahead, amidst much politeness and good cheer, the Spanish lines and camp were visited by senior British officers and, in turn, Gibraltar visited by Mshl de Crillon and his staff. The marshal was very impressed at what he saw and, at Ince's Gallery, is said to have exclaimed: 'These works are worthy of the Romans!'

Indeed, the defence of Gibraltar between 1779 and 1783 was worthy of the great classics in the Art of War, ancient and modern.

WESTERN MEDITERRANEAN AFTER THE SIEGE

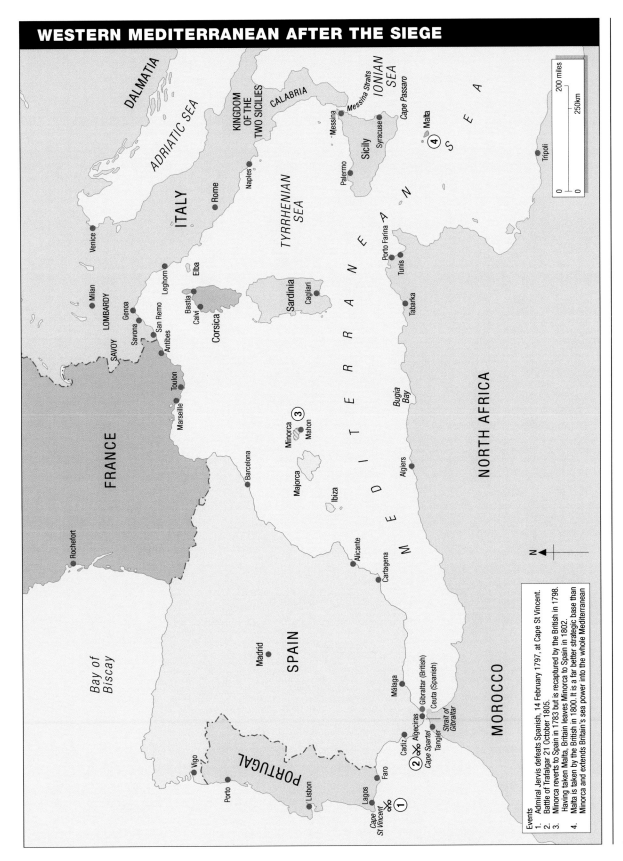

DALMATIA

ADRIATIC SEA

KINGDOM OF THE TWO SICILIES

CALABRIA

Messina Straits

IONIAN SEA

Cape Passaro

Messina

Malta

④

Syracuse

Sicily

Palermo

Tripoli

ITALY

Rome

Naples

TYRRHENIAN SEA

M E D I T E R R A N E A N

Venice

Milan

LOMBARDY

Genoa

Savona

San Remo

Antibes

Leghorn

Elba

Bastia

Calvi

Corsica

Sardinia

Cagliari

Porto Farina

Tunis

Tabarka

SAVOY

Toulon

Marseille

FRANCE

Rochefort

Bugia Bay

Algiers

NORTH AFRICA

Minorca

③

Mahon

Barcelona

Majorca

Ibiza

Alicante

Cartagena

Málaga

Gibraltar (British)

Ceuta (Spanish)

Strait of Gibraltar

Algeciras

②

Tangier

Cape Spartel

Cadiz

MOROCCO

Madrid

SPAIN

Bay of Biscay

Vigo

Porto

PORTUGAL

Lisbon

Lagos

Faro

Cape St Vincent

①

N

200 miles
250km

Events

1. Admiral Jervis defeats Spanish, 14 February 1797, at Cape St Vincent.
2. Battle of Trafalgar 21 October 1805.
3. Minorca reverts to Spain in 1783 but is recaptured by the British in 1798. Having taken Malta, Britain leaves Minorca to Spain in 1802.
4. Malta is taken by the British in 1800. It is a far better strategic base than Minorca and extends Britain's sea power into the whole Mediterranean

AFTERMATH

From the later part of 1782, Lord Shelburne headed the British government. His prime aim was to negotiate a peace treaty. All belligerents were, by then, somewhat exhausted by the war. King George III and most of the cabinet were disposed to let go of Gibraltar if an adequate compensation were found. In Madrid, King Carlos III was very keen on finally obtaining the Rock. At the peace negotiations, there was talk of exchanging Gibraltar for Puerto Rico and West Florida but, following a flurry of messages back and forth between Madrid and London, the Spanish found this to be too much. West Florida had been their big success in the war. Worse, Puerto Rico was the entry point to the Spanish Main and to cede it to the British was tantamount to inviting disaster in a future war.

In Britain, there was increasing unease about Gibraltar in the government as it was realized that British public opinion was over-whelmingly against such a deal. The war had been disastrous, with the American colonies lost, many West Indian islands taken by the French and the East Indies under threat; only the outstanding resistance of Gibraltar confirmed British valour. By late November, King Carlos was most reluctantly envisaging peace without Gibraltar, the only remaining major issue. The Count de Vergennes, France's foreign minister, then pushed the issue – some say he double-crossed the Spanish king – for peace if all of Florida and Minorca went to Spain. The British readily agreed. The preliminaries of peace, which called for a ceasefire, were signed on 20 January 1783 and the final treaty at Versailles on 3 September of that year. Ultimately, nothing was said about Gibraltar in the treaty. The Rock therefore remained British.

In the years following the Great Siege, life at the Rock settled into the quiet routine of a garrison while the town was reconstructed. Tensions rose with the aftermath of the French Revolution that, once again, put

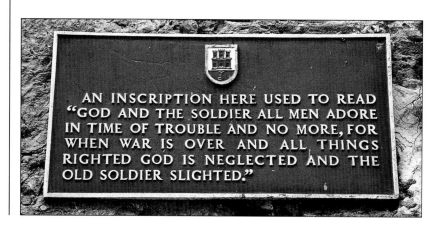

Plaque relating a remarkable 18th-century 'soldier's text' found inscribed on the wall near Prince Edward's Gate at Gibraltar. (Author's photo)

Britain at war with Spain and France. No siege was attempted but, in 1798, a huge conspiracy to hand over Gibraltar to Spain was uncovered involving Spanish Prime Minister Godoy, Jewish businessmen in Paris and Gibraltar and some reluctant Irish officers in the garrison. A purge followed in the garrison and some 1,100 residents were told to leave. The British government was not about to lose its prime Mediterranean base to a plot. Indeed, that same year, the expedition that re-took Minorca from the Spanish sailed from the Rock.

Possibly the most tense and exciting times during that period for the garrison and residents of Gibraltar came in 1801. On the night of 12 July, a Spanish fleet that included two 112-gun ships at Algeciras tried to break out into the open sea; they were engaged in the dark by the smaller but much faster HMS *Superb* out of Gibraltar that sailed between the two large Spanish ships, firing broadsides from both sides in the dark. As the Royal Navy ship sailed on, the confused Spaniards fired at each other, collided, burst into flames and went down with some 1,700 men. The following year, the Treaty of Amiens returned Minorca to Spain, but Britain now had a much better base: the island fortress of Malta, off the Italian coast.

War was again declared with Spain in December 1804 and, on 21 October 1805, the last of the Franco-Spanish fleet's might was destroyed by Adm Nelson off Cape Trafalgar, west of Gibraltar. HMS *Victory* as well as other British ships found refuge in Gibraltar from the violent storm that rose after the battle. The Spanish loosely blockaded the Rock until 1808 when, in a dramatic turn of events, all of Spain rose against the French when Napoleon took the Spanish throne for his brother Joseph. From despised enemies, the British and Spanish suddenly became allies in a life-and-death struggle against Napoleon's almighty Continental empire. With the Portuguese, they waged the Peninsular War for six years against the French and their allies. Gibraltar was never directly involved, although regiments and supplies from the Rock went into Spain.

The end of the Napoleonic Wars brought a very long quiet period for Gibraltar. During that time, the British continued to improve the fortifications of the Rock, notably by making some 7 miles (12 km) of tunnels in it, as Spain's claims to it never ceased. But it had become a symbol of Britain's might and naval preponderance as well as a valuable strategic base, and the British people were emotionally attached to it.

The Great War of 1914–18 brought its share of tensions but Spain was neutral in the struggle. It was political events in Spain that brought renewed worries. The leftist Spanish republic was proclaimed in 1932 and, four years later, part of the Spanish Army rose against the government and a devastating civil war ensued. The republicans were backed by left-leaning democrats, communists and the Soviet Union, while the nationalists had help from right-wing movements and fascist regimes in Benito Mussolini's Italy and Adolph Hitler's Germany. Britain remained neutral but tensions rose in Gibraltar. The importance of air power became obvious during this bitter war and the first air raid shelters were built in Gibraltar from 1936. The Spanish Civil War ended in 1939 with the triumph of General Franco's nationalists who installed a fascist regime.

From September 1939, Britain was at war with Germany and, from June 1940, with Italy. Spain remained neutral, but this was a period of outstanding tensions for the Rock. The greatest menace came from Hitler's 'Operation *Felix*' – a plan to take Gibraltar spawned from **89**

Soldier-Artificer Company of Gibraltar. Raised in 1772, the company's early uniform is said to have been a red coat with orange-yellow facings, brass buttons stamped with the coat of arms of the Board of Ordnance, white waistcoat and blue breeches, these latter being changed to white by 1786 as shown in this print by Campion in Connolly's 1855 *History of the Corps of Royal Sappers and Miners*. (Author's photo)

HMS *Victory* being towed into Gibraltar by HMS *Neptune* after the battle of Trafalgar in October 1805, which was fought to the north-west between Cadiz and Gibraltar. After the battle, the British fleet found shelter from a violent storm at the Rock's harbour. HMS *Victory* was brought in for some repairs at Rosia Bay, possibly the most famous ship ever to dock there. It had often been to Gibraltar before, most notably with Adm Howe's relief fleet in October 1782. (Print after Henry Charles Miller. Author's photo)

July 1940. There is little doubt that a strong and well-equipped German corps with air support might have taken Gibraltar, but this involved travelling from France across Spain on very poor roads and almost no infrastructure with secrecy being totally out of the question. Spanish collaboration was necessary but, at their meeting in October, Franco made it clear to Hitler that he would not go to war. As much as he wanted Gibraltar, his country had been utterly devastated by the civil war. Thereafter, Hitler's attention turned to the Soviet Union; in February 1941, Operation *Felix* was cancelled; Gibraltar had escaped another siege. Meanwhile, the fall of France and Italy's entry into the war since June 1940 had raised concerns for Gibraltar's population and its 18,000 civilians were evacuated to Britain, Madeira and Jamaica until the end of hostilities. The Royal Engineers kept digging in the Rock, adding another 16 miles of tunnels during the war to this vitally important base to the Mediterranean. This work went on after 1945 and there are now said to be about 35 miles (50 km) of tunnels in the Rock.

The post-war era was relatively quiet, with various political options being considered by Gibraltarians in a period of decolonization. In 1967, a referendum revealed only 44 people favouring union with Spain and

ABOVE **Gibraltar seen from the farthest point of the Spanish lines during Spain's 1968–85 blockade. There was a lot of Spanish military activity at La Línea at the time the author took this photo in 1981 while nothing much could be seen beyond a 'no man's land' except, in the distance, the buildings at the British airfield. But everyone, and especially the Spanish, had the awkward feeling of never seeing the British while knowing that, up in the caves of the Rock, observers saw everything at Spain's border. (Author's photo)**

RIGHT **Gibraltar from La Línea, Spain, in 2003. Spain naturally still claims Gibraltar; indeed, it has become something of a Spanish national pastime. But adhesion to the European Union has certainly challenged attitudes since the end of the blockade in 1985 and a broad boulevard now leads to Gibraltar. There are still Customs at each side of the border; Gibraltar is a tax-free zone and Spaniards shop there without paying VAT while Gibraltarians do the same in Spain, thus avoiding the Rock's local sales tax, all of which is supposed to be declared at their respective Customs. (Author's photo)**

RIGHT **Every Saturday, the 'Ceremony of the keys' is performed by re-enactors in period uniforms at Casemate Square, to the delight of visitors. The casemates there were built in 1817. The uniforms approximate those worn by the Rock's valiant garrison during the Great Siege. (Author's photo)**

12,138 against. However, Spain had not given up its claim on Gibraltar and, to this day, every Spaniard feels, as a matter of national pride, that the place is Spanish territory usurped by the British. General Franco, who had become the 'Caudillo' – protector/dictator – of Spain, thought so, too. On 6 May 1968, the Spanish government closed the frontier of Gibraltar and started a blockade. The only entrance to Gibraltar was via Morocco. It was hoped to ruin if not starve out the place and pressure the British into negotiating a transfer. Whatever sympathy there might have been among Gibraltarians for an eventual political arrangement with Spain vanished and, from what this author gathered on the spot, this option seems most unlikely to be entertained again for several generations. Not only was trust in anything the Spanish government would say or do utterly broken, but also the Rock's economic ruin did not occur. Instead, at least 7,000 Spanish workers lost their employment in Gibraltar, some of their jobs going to Moroccans.

The death of Franco in 1975 and the advent of democratic government in Spain did not immediately change anything for Gibraltar. However, Spain wished to join the European Union and, for that to happen, the blockade would have to end. On 5 February 1985, the border with Spain was reopened after 16 years.

In the first decade of the 21st century, in 2004, Gibraltar celebrated its 300th year under the Union Jack .

THE BATTLEFIELD TODAY

Most visitors going into Gibraltar in the early 21st century arrive there after a pleasant drive through southern Spain. The Rock is visible from a long way off and its impressive bulk becomes overwhelming as one drives up the highway going through the Neutral Grounds. There are still border stations manned by Spanish and British Customs guards as Gibraltar is, like Jersey and several other territories in Europe, a free economic zone. Once inside Gibraltar, everything seems different from Spain. The architecture is reminiscent of British tropical territories such as the West Indies, there are many pubs and even helmeted 'bobbies' as in London. The streets are very cosmopolitan, with Spaniards, Moroccans, Britons and, of course, Gibraltarians looking for bargains in the many shops advertising tax-free items. The shallow- water

A view within the 'Great Siege Tunnel' built from July 1782 by SgtMaj Ince and his artificers. The place today is practically identical to when it was built. (Author's photo)

areas facing the town into the bay have been filled and built up with businesses and apartments; the seashore in the days of the Great Siege is now covered with roads and buildings. There is even a large Muslim mosque recently built at Europa Point by an oil-rich Arab country.

Those wishing to see fortifications will not be disappointed. They are very much in evidence and well preserved, from the Moorish Castle to the more recent works. A visit to the 'Great Siege Tunnels', as Ince's Gallery is called, is an essential experience. The Gibraltar Museum has many objects of interest, including an 1865 Royal Engineers model of the Rock. A ride up to the top of the Rock is also a must and offers a superb and unique viewpoint of the area and of the walls. (If you take food out of the restaurant up there, beware of the monkeys, who will appear from nowhere and take it from your tray with lightning speed!) There is excellent ordnance still mounted in several outer batteries at the New Mole and Rosia Bay, including a rare 100-ton Armstrong gun. Even a visit to the public gardens will be rewarded with viewing brass mortars and monuments, including one to Governor Eliott, the 'Cock of the Rock'. His spirit still haunts and inspires Gibraltar, a place that is, in many a Briton's heart, an extension of the White Cliffs of Dover.

The town of Gibraltar from the top of the rock. There has been considerable development in the last 20 years and the town's surface has been expanded by extensive land reclamation on its western shore. (Author's photo)

SELECT BIBLIOGRAPHY

There is an abundant number of published sources and studies in English regarding the Great Siege. The best known and possibly the most complete contemporary account is Captain John Drinkwater's *History of the Late Siege of Gibraltar* (London, 1785), which is illustrated with good maps and plates. It has been our main guide and source. Captain Spilsbury's *A Journal of the Siege of Gibraltar 1779–1783* (Gibraltar, 1908) is a shorter account with many interesting plates by its author. Francis Duncan's *History of the Royal Regiment of Artillery*, Vol. 1 (London, 1879) and T.W.J. Connolly's *History of the Royal Sappers & Miners*, Vol. 1 (London, 1855) both contain good accounts of their respective arms. Although many studies quote Governor Eliott's letters, they have never been published in their entirety but all may be read at the Public Records Office at Kew, UK (recently renamed 'The National Archive', a title used by archives in many countries. Therefore, to avoid confusion, we continue to use 'PRO'). The pertinent correspondence is in Colonial Office 91, volumes 25 to 29. Inspection returns in War Office 1, 27 and 34 have also been consulted. The PRO also has a good collection of maps and plans.

Of the modern studies, Jack Russel's *Gibraltar Besieged* (London, 1965) and T.H. McGuffie's *The Siege of Gibraltar* (London, 1965) are recommended. The sieges of Minorca and Gibraltar are related in the context of the war in Vol. 3 of Sir John W. Fortescue's *History of the British Army* (London, 1902). Nor should the late 19th-century anonymous study *Gibraltar and its Sieges* not be considered. Sir Charles Petrie's *King Charles III of Spain* (New York, 1971) gives a good account of Spain's objectives. The *Gibtel Gibraltar Heritage Journal* has useful data as does George Palao's booklet *The Guns and Towers of Gibraltar* (Gibraltar, 1975). Maurice Harvey's *Gibraltar: a history* (Staplehurst, 1996) is an essential and well-illustrated reference. Britain's naval situation in that era is admirably given in N.A.M. Rodger's *The Command of the Ocean* (London, 2004).

Spanish and French sources and studies on the Great Siege are understandably rarer. Both the Duc de Crillon and the Chevalier D'Arçon published memoirs and accounts after the war but they are naturally apologetic and vague on the performance of the combined forces. Crillon's son fortunately left a lively correspondence published in *La Sabretache* during 1907. Although the Spanish forces were heavily involved, there seems to have been few studies on their services during the Great Siege that are readily accessible in Spain. Conde de Clonard's *Historia orgánica de la infantería y caballería Española* (Madrid, *c.* 1850s), Vol. 5, and Francisco Barado's *Historia del Ejército Español* (Barcelona, *c.* 1895), Vol. 3, have interesting chapters on the event as does the more recent *España y el mar en el siglo de Carlos III* (Madrid, 1989) and José Cervera Pery's *La Marina de la Ilustración* (Madrid, 1986). *La Toma de Menorca 1782* (Madrid, 2005) offers a Spanish view of the siege of Minorca.

INDEX